Rock Recipes
CHRISTMAS

YOUR COMPLETE GUIDE TO A DELICIOUS HOLIDAY SEASON

BARRY C. PARSONS

BREAKWATER
P.O. Box 2188 | St. John's | NL | Canada | A1C 6E6
www.breakwaterbooks.com

A CIP catalogue record for this book is available from Library and Archives Canada.

ISBN 978-1-55081-655-6 (bound)
Copyright © 2016 Barry C. Parsons

Canadä

Newfoundland Labrador

We acknowledge the financial support of the Government of Canada and the Government of Newfoundland and Labrador through the Department of Tourism, Culture and Recreation for our publishing activities.

PRINTED AND BOUND IN CANADA

Breakwater Books is committed to choosing papers and materials for our books that help to protect our environment. To this end, this book is printed on a recycled paper that is certified by the Forest Stewardship Council of Canada.

For

MEB AND THE OLE CROW
(A.K.A. MOM AND DAD)

who always worked hard to make sure Christmas
was perfect for six overexcited kids.

132

96

164

70

CONTENTS

Growing up in Newfoundland in the 1970s and 1980s, Christmas was everything it should have been. It was a time of great excitement and anticipation for the six children in our family. As anyone who comes from a larger family can tell you, the more kids in the family, the more exponential that excitement and anticipation grows. By Christmas Eve our home was a madhouse of eager energy as one kid's excitement amplified that of the next.

We must have been very good girls and boys just the same, because Santa never disappointed, bringing each of us the object of our heart's desire each year—from a new bicycle to the latest fad toy for the younger kids. Of course, asking for a bike for Christmas in Newfoundland is like ordering up another six months of tortured anticipation until you can properly use it. None of us made that mistake twice.

As much as I never wanted for anything on the material side of Christmas, it is really the celebration with family and friends that I remember most, and great food was always a huge part of the festivities. It seemed to me back then that everyone you knew visited everyone they ever knew during the holiday season. The twelve days of Christmas were spent in marathon sessions of visiting relatives and friends for endless cold plates, massive pots of turkey soup, and of course all those Christmas baked treats.

I've written many times about the prolific and talented bakers in my family from whom I learned so much. The Christmas season for them was the absolute zenith of the baking year when all the stops were pulled out and preparations began weeks in advance. Cupboards were filled with carefully wrapped Christmas cakes, sealed inside huge cake tins. Freezer doors could barely shut, having been stogged with hundreds of Christmas cookies. All the while, during this yearly production, the smell of something delicious in the oven never abated; the scent wafting through the house as if to announce the arrival of the coming feast.

When it came to food for the holidays, there were always family favourites that were must-haves each year, but there were always one or two new additions as recipes for cookies and cakes in particular were traded among family and friends. This Christmas cookbook is both a celebration of Christmases past and an encouragement to discover something new to add to your own celebrations. Keeping the best of the old and adding a sprinkling of the new has long been my recipe for a successful and delicious Christmas season.

Whether it's re-acquainting with a delicious memory from the past, putting a new twist on a classic, or discovering a whole new favourite to add to your own Christmas traditions, I hope this book serves to help make your holiday season just a little more enjoyable.

CHRISTMAS
BAKING

In my family, the biggest part of preparing for Christmas is definitely the baking. It was when I was a child, and it still is now that I have children of my own, as it is in many households in Newfoundland today. Traditional favourites like molasses raisin bread for Christmas Eve or rum-soaked dark fruitcake to be enjoyed in small slices throughout the season, are still always made in my home, as are many family-favourite cookie squares. Some of the most popular of those recipes are included here along with some incredibly decadent desserts for those special dinners throughout the holidays. There are plenty of ideas here to fill your freezers and cupboards with the tastiest treats Christmas has to offer.

APRICOT ALMOND JAMMIE DODGERS

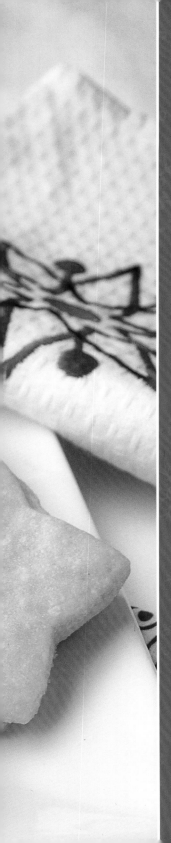

COOKIES

Fruitcake Cookies

PREP TIME: **15** MINUTES + CHILLING TIME | COOK TIME: **12** MINUTES | MAKES **24** COOKIES

¾ cup soft, room-temperature butter

½ cup packed brown sugar

½ cup white sugar

¼ cup molasses

1 egg

2 cups flour

2 tsp baking soda

½ tsp salt

1½ tsp ground cinnamon

½ tsp ground cloves

1½ tsp ground ginger

½ cup chopped glacé cherries

½ cup chopped dates

½ cup mixed glacé citrus peel (or glacé fruit mix)

½ cup roughly chopped toasted pecans or walnuts (optional)

This dough freezes well, so you can roll them into balls and freeze them, then take them out of the freezer, let thaw for 30 minutes and bake as usual. They may take an extra 1-2 minutes in the oven this way, but you can make as many or as few as you like.

When it comes to fruitcake, there's no grey area. You're either a fan or you're not. Most fruitcake detractors are pretty adamant about their positions, but these cookies have been known to make some pause and reconsider. When you experience all the flavour of a traditional molasses-and-spice dark fruitcake, translated into a crispy, chewy cookie, even the most ardent fruitcake opponents can become cookie converts.

1. In the bowl of an electric mixer, mix together the butter, sugars, and molasses until well blended.

2. Beat in the egg for an additional minute.

3. Combine the flour, baking soda, salt, cinnamon, cloves, and ginger and fold into the molasses mixture. Fold in all of the fruit and nuts if you are using them. Cover and chill dough for a couple of hours or overnight.

4. Preheat oven to 350°F.

5. Roll dough into 1-inch sized balls. Place cookies 2½ inches apart onto ungreased baking sheets lined with parchment paper or silicone baking liners. Press down slightly with the bottom of a water glass. You can dip the water glass in a little flour to prevent it from sticking to the dough.

6. Bake for 10 to 12 minutes in the preheated oven. Allow to rest on the cookie sheet for a few minutes before transferring them to wire racks to cool.

Haystacks

Haystack Cookies are a very quick and easy version of a macaroons recipe using just a few simple ingredients. I always get requests for this recipe during the holiday season because they are a real old-fashioned Newfoundland favourite at Christmas. It seemed every baker I knew while growing up made these every year.

1 cup sweetened condensed milk

2 tsp vanilla extract

pinch salt

5 cups unsweetened dried coconut (fine or medium cut)

2 large egg whites

3 tbsp sugar

¼ tsp cream of tartar

¼ cup glacé cherries

1. Preheat oven to 325°F.

2. Line baking sheet(s) with parchment paper.

3. Combine the sweetened condensed milk, the vanilla extract, and salt. Fold in the coconut.

4. Whip the egg whites to soft peaks along with the sugar and cream of tartar.

5. Fold the egg whites completely through the coconut mixture.

6. Form the haystacks using a boiled egg cup or small ice-cream scoop. Keeping the inside of the egg cup slightly wet helps form the cookies.

7. Top each haystack with a piece of glacé cherry or other dried fruits or nuts.

8. Bake for about 20-25 minutes or until the bottom edges just begin to turn brown.

9. Cool completely on the pan. Store in an airtight container. The cookies can be frozen too.

Chocolate Orange Cookies

PREP TIME: **20** MINUTES + CHILLING TIME | COOK TIME: **15** MINUTES | MAKES **12** LARGE COOKIES

1⅓ cups flour

½ tsp salt

½ tsp baking soda

½ cup butter

½ cup light brown sugar

½ cup sugar

1 egg

1 tsp vanilla extract

1½ cups roughly chopped Terry's Chocolate Orange

To freeze individual portions of cookie dough, roll the dough in about 1½-inch balls and lay them on a piece of parchment paper or waxed paper on a cookie sheet then press down slightly with the heel of your hand. Freeze them completely before storing them in an airtight container. Separate the layers of cookie dough balls with waxed paper or parchment paper. To bake, place the frozen portions on a parchment lined cookie sheet and let them thaw at room temperature for 20-30 minutes before baking.

Every year without fail, Spouse puts one of those delicious, round chocolate oranges in my stocking for Christmas morning. They originated in the UK, and everyone in our family loves them. It just wouldn't be Christmas without them. One Christmas a few years ago, I tried making chocolate chunk cookies out of them, and everyone raved about how delicious they were. They've been on every one of my Christmas cookie lists since and are often made several times during the Christmas season to be served warm out of the oven to appreciative guests.

1. Preheat oven to 350°F.

2. Line cookie sheets with parchment paper.

3. In a medium-sized bowl, whisk together flour, salt, and baking soda.

4. In a large bowl, cream together the butter and sugars until light and fluffy.

5. Add the egg and vanilla and combine thoroughly.

6. Add the flour mixture to the sweetened butter. Mix only enough to incorporate flour. Do not overmix. Fold in the chunks of Terry's Chocolate Orange.

7. It is best to chill this dough very well before baking. This helps to prevent them spreading too much on the pan as they bake.

8. Form cookies by dropping a rounded tablespoon of dough on the prepared cookie sheet 3 inches apart. I like to reserve a few pieces of chocolate to poke into the top of the cookie dough portions which makes them even more visually appealing. Bake until light brown around the edges, about 12-15 minutes, depending on cookie size. For larger cookies like these, I usually only bake about 6 per sheet.

9. Overbaking is the biggest problem with most chocolate chunk cookies. Your oven's temperature accuracy and the type of cookie sheet you use will vary the baking times considerably. When they are golden brown around the edges, it's time to remove them from the oven. Thinking they are a little underdone is probably a good thing. Experiment by baking only a couple of cookies at a time to see what the perfect baking time is for your oven.

10. Cool for 10 minutes on the baking sheet before removing to a wire rack to cool thoroughly.

Old-Fashioned Shortbread Cookies

PREP TIME: **15** MINUTES + CHILLING TIME | COOK TIME: **15** MINUTES | MAKES **24** COOKIES

2 cups **butter** at room temperature

1 cup **icing sugar** (powdered sugar)

2 tsp **vanilla extract**

½ cup **cornstarch**

3 cups **flour**

maraschino cherries or **baking gums** for the centers (optional)

I have been a lifelong fan of the perfect simplicity of well-made, buttery shortbread cookies. I've tried many different kinds of shortbread over the years, from espresso flavoured to tutti frutti, but at the holidays, when harkening back to childhood Christmases, this old-fashioned favourite still shines as one of the best. Although many may already have a very similar version of this recipe, I include it as a reminder that when baking for those closest to you at Christmas, sometimes the simple things are best and most appreciated.

1. Cream together the butter and icing sugar well until very smooth and creamy. No lumps of butter should be visible.

2. Blend in the vanilla extract.

3. Sift together the flour and cornstarch then blend slowly into the creamed mixture until a soft dough forms.

4. Split dough into 2 equal round portions.

5. Wrap the dough rounds in plastic wrap and chill for a couple of hours at least. You can freeze one of the cookie dough portions for later if you like. This dough will also last in the fridge for 3-4 days so you can bake a few up at a time and enjoy them fresh from the oven whenever you want.

6. Preheat the oven to 350°F and line cookie sheets with parchment paper.

7. Roll the dough out to a little less than ¼ of an inch on a lightly floured surface. Use a 2-inch cookie cutter (or holiday-shaped cookie cutters) to cut out the cookies.

8. Place the cookies on the parchment paper ½ inch apart. Add a half maraschino or glacé cherry to the center, or a baking gumdrop if you like.

9. Bake for 15-20 minutes or until they just start to turn brown at the edges.

10. Let cool for 10 minutes on the pan before transferring them to a wire rack to cool completely. Store in an airtight container. These cookies will freeze quite well for several weeks.

Tweedies

Tweed Squares, or Tweedies as they are known in our family, are a much-loved Newfoundland favourite and a treat many people remember their mothers and grandmothers making. More like a small piece of cake than a cookie bar, these delicious, chocolate-flecked squares are one of my earliest memories of home baking. They remain a Christmas must-have in our house because they are my son Noah's favourite. That's one more generation of Tweedie lovers guaranteed already.

CAKE BASE

1½ cup flour

2 tsp baking powder

½ tsp salt

½ cup butter

⅔ cup sugar

2 egg yolks (reserve whites)

½ cup milk

1 oz dark chocolate, finely grated

VANILLA FROSTING

⅓ cup butter

1½ cups icing sugar (powdered sugar)

1 tsp vanilla extract

a little milk

CHOCOLATE TOPPING

1 cup chocolate chips

2 tbsp butter

CAKE BASE

1. Grease and flour a 9x9-inch baking pan well or line with parchment paper.

2. Preheat oven to 325°F.

3. Sift together the flour, baking powder, and salt and set aside.

4. Cream together the butter and sugar well. Add the egg yolks and beat until creamy.

5. Fold in the flour alternately with the milk, beginning and ending with the dry ingredients. Do not overmix.

6. Beat the egg whites to soft peaks and gently fold them into the cake batter. When the egg whites are almost incorporated fold in the grated chocolate.

7. Pour batter into the prepared pan and bake for about 20-25 minutes or until a toothpick inserted in the center comes out clean. Be careful not to overbake the cake portion. Cool completely on a wire rack. Top with vanilla frosting.

For a thinner cake base, try this recipe in a 9x13-inch pan and adding 1½ times the recipe for the filling and topping. Just be careful not to overbake the cake or it can be dry. If your cake domes too much in the pan, you can always cut a little off the top horizontally with a serrated knife before adding the frosting layer.

VANILLA FROSTING

1. Cream together the butter, icing sugar, and vanilla. You may add a little milk 1 teaspoon at a time, if the frosting seems too stiff to be spreadable, but the frosting should be quite a thick consistency; much thicker than cake frosting.

2. Spread evenly on the baked cake base and chill in the fridge for a couple of hours before adding the chocolate topping.

CHOCOLATE TOPPING

1. Melt the chocolate and butter together over low heat or in a double boiler.

2. Cool to lukewarm and spread quickly over the chilled frosting. Let the chocolate set before cutting into squares or bars and serving. These also freeze quite well.

Easy Lemon Bars

PREP TIME: **20** MINUTES | COOK TIME: **40** MINUTES | MAKES ABOUT **36** BARS

So what's so Christmassy about lemon bars? Well, the truth is, in the very last few days before Christmas, and often even on Christmas Day, this uncomplicated recipe jumps to the most viewed position on *RockRecipes.com*. I always imagine people scrambling to get something—anything—that's home baked in the house before Santa comes down the chimney. With only five ingredients, a very simple preparation method, and a huge payout in flavour for such little effort, I'd say those last-minute folks chose well. If you make these lemon bars in the last few days before Christmas, you may just find yourself making them year round.

PASTRY

1 cup **cold butter**, cut in small pieces

½ cup **sugar**

2 cups **flour**

LEMON LAYER

1½ cups **sugar**

¼ cup **flour**

4 **eggs**

zest of 2 **lemons**, very finely chopped

juice of 2 **lemons** (about ⅔ to ¾ cup juice)

PASTRY

1. Preheat oven to 350°F (325°F if using glass bakeware).

2. Using a pastry cutter or in a food processor, blend together the butter, sugar, and flour.

3. Press evenly into the bottom of a greased and parchment-lined 9×13-inch baking pan.

4. Bake for 20-25 minutes. The bottom should just be beginning to brown slightly at the top edges.

LEMON LAYER

1. Simply whisk together the sugar, flour, eggs, zest, and lemon juice until the sugar is dissolved.

2. Allow the topping to sit for about 10 minutes before whisking together well again and pouring over the baked shortbread base.

3. Bake at 350°F for about another 20-25 minutes or until the top is slightly browned and the lemon custard appears to be set.

4. Cool completely. Using a fine sieve, sprinkle with icing sugar when cool.

Snowballs

PREP TIME: **15** MINUTES + CHILLING TIME | COOK TIME: **5** MINUTES

MAKES ABOUT **4** DOZEN

Every year at Christmas, practically everyone in our extended family makes my Nan Morgan's recipe for snowballs. It just wouldn't be Christmas without them. Much akin to making fudge, a snowball should be soft. If you over-boil the mixture, the sugar will crystallize and your snowballs will become hard and crumbly. Snowballs freeze very well and hold up in the freezer longer than some other Christmas treats, so they're always a good choice to be the first thing you make to start your holiday preparations. You just may need a lock for your freezer though if you want to avoid making multiple batches in the run up to Christmas.

3 cups sugar

¾ cup melted butter

1¼ cups milk

3 cups large rolled oats

1 cup unsweetened fine coconut

¾ cup cocoa

1.   In a large saucepan, combine the sugar, melted butter, and milk and boil together gently over medium-high heat for 5 minutes or until mixture reaches about 225-230°F on a candy thermometer. Once mixture begins to boil, it's very important not to stir it at all.

2.   Mix together the rolled oats, coconut, and cocoa. Add the boiled mixture to the dry ingredients until well-combined, and chill well until the mixture is able to be shaped into 1½-inch balls. Roll the balls in additional coconut. These should be stored in the fridge, and they freeze very well (my kids eat them frozen all the time, just like my siblings and I did when we were young).

Five Star Bars

PREP TIME: **10** MINUTES | COOK TIME: **20** MINUTES | MAKES **24** BARS

¼ cup **melted butter**

2 cups **graham cracker crumbs**

2 cups **unsweetened coconut**

10 oz **sweetened condensed milk**

1 tsp **vanilla**

1 cup **chocolate chips** (milk chocolate, semi-sweet, or dark)

This recipe always sees a surge in views on my website in the weeks before the holidays. Five Star Bars are more a confection than a cookie bar, with coconut and graham crumbs suspended in a chewy caramel-like base that's then topped with chocolate. They are a local favourite here in Newfoundland and are made in many local bakeries across the province. Since these also freeze very well, they are an excellent choice for the Christmas freezer.

1. Preheat oven to 350°F.

2. Mix together the butter, graham crumbs, coconut, condensed milk, and vanilla.

3. Press into a parchment-lined 9x9-inch pan.

4. Bake for 20 minutes or until firm.

5. As soon as they come out of the oven, sprinkle the chocolate chips over the top of the hot cookie bars.

6. Let stand for 5-10 minutes to allow the chocolate to melt, then spread evenly over the top.

7. Allow the bars to cool to room temperature before cutting.

8. Store in an airtight container. These cookie bars freeze well too.

Queen Anne Squares

BOTTOM LAYER

⅔ cup **melted butter**

⅔ cup **brown sugar**

1 cup **flour**

4 tbsp **cocoa**

1 tsp **vanilla extract**

1 **extra large egg**

COCONUT LAYER

1 can **sweetened condensed milk**

2 cups **dried coconut**

1 tsp **vanilla extract**

CHOCOLATE FROSTING

2 cups **icing sugar** (powdered sugar)

3 tbsp **cocoa**

1 tsp **vanilla**

2 or 3 tbsp **milk**

¼ cup **butter**

This is another local bakery favourite in Newfoundland, but many people bake their own for the holidays. I tweaked the original old church cookbook version of this recipe from many years ago to make it a little richer and chocolatey. The sweetened condensed milk ensures that the coconut does not dry out like in some recipes. My version gets rave reviews from even long-time fans of this popular treat.

BOTTOM LAYER

1. Beat together the melted butter, brown sugar, flour, cocoa, vanilla extract, and egg until smooth.

2. Spread evenly into the bottom of a lightly greased and parchment-lined 9x9-inch baking pan.

COCONUT LAYER

1. Preheat oven to 350°F.

2. Mix together the condensed milk, coconut, and vanilla extract until completely blended then drop by heaping teaspoonful onto the cake batter layer. Spread out carefully.

3. Bake for 25 minutes. Cool completely before adding the chocolate frosting on top.

CHOCOLATE FROSTING

1. Beat together the icing sugar, cocoa, vanilla, milk, and butter until smooth. Add only enough milk to bring the frosting to a smooth but spreadable consistency. A frosting that is a bit on the thick consistency side works best here.

2. Spread on the cooled cookies and cut into squares or bars.

Tutti Frutti Shortbread Cookies

PREP TIME: **15** MINUTES + CHILLING TIME | COOK TIME: **15** MINUTES | MAKES **4** DOZEN

2 cups **unsalted butter**

¾ cup **sugar**

2 tsp **pure vanilla extract**

4 cups **flour**

½ tsp **salt**

1½ cups **mixed glacé fruit**

These very festive looking treats use so few ingredients to make such buttery flavourful cookies. Based on a Scottish shortbread recipe, they freeze well or can be treated as "bake-off" cookies, keeping the dough logs in the fridge for several days, slicing off as many as you need and baking them to serve fresh from the oven. Nothing welcomes people to your home during the holidays like the aroma of freshly baked cookies greeting them on their arrival.

1. Cream together the butter, sugar, and vanilla until very light and fluffy.

2. Gently fold in the flour and salt until the dry ingredients are almost completely incorporated.

3. Add the glacé fruit and work into a soft dough.

4. Form the dough into two 1½-inch wide logs.

5. Wrap the dough logs in plastic wrap and chill for a couple of hours. (Note: This dough will be fine in the fridge for several days if you want to bake off the cookies a few at a time as needed.)

6. Preheat oven to 350°F.

7. Using a very sharp knife, cut ¼-inch slices of dough from the log and place 2 inches apart on a parchment-lined baking sheet.

8. Bake for about 15-18 minutes until the bottom edges are noticeably golden brown.

9. Transfer to a wire rack to cool completely. Store in an airtight container. These cookies also freeze very well. And you can drizzle these with melted white chocolate if you like.

Date Crumbles

PREP TIME: 20 MINUTES + CHILLING TIME | COOK TIME: 40 MINUTES | MAKES ABOUT 36 SQUARES

Whether you call them Date Crumbles or Date Squares, there can be little doubt that these have been the most popular cookie bars in Newfoundland for decades. It's one of those things that someone in everyone's family bakes, especially at Christmas time. What may set this recipe apart from others is the ample amount of filling and the use of plenty of butter to help hold the crumble together and give it a fuller, richer flavour. I've tried many date crumbles in my day but none better than this recipe produces.

FILLING

18 oz dates, chopped

3 tbsp butter

3 tbsp sugar

1½ tbsp vanilla

2 cups boiling water

CRUMBLE

2 cups rolled oats (large, and not quick oats)

2 tsp baking powder

1 cup unsweetened coconut

2 cups flour

1 cup brown sugar

1½ cups butter, cut in small cubes

FILLING

1.   In a medium saucepan, combine all of the ingredients for the filling and gently simmer until thickened (about 10-15 minutes). The filling should be very thick and paste-like; you will need to watch it carefully and stir constantly in the last few minutes of cooking time.

2.   Set aside to cool slightly while you prepare the crumble mixture.

CRUMBLE

1.   Preheat oven to 350°F.

2.   Lightly grease a 9x13-inch baking pan and line with parchment paper if you want.

3.   In a large bowl, toss together the rolled oats, baking powder, coconut, flour, and brown sugar.

4.   Using your hands, rub the butter thoroughly through the dry ingredients.

5.   Divide crumble mixture in half and press half into the bottom of the prepared baking pan.

6.   Spread date mixture over the base.

7.   Top with remaining crumb mixture, pressing it together in clumps in your hands and then breaking it into small pieces with your fingers to scatter evenly over the date filling. Press down lightly, and bake for 40 minutes.

This is a great basic recipe, but I've developed amazing variations of date crumbles over the years.

Orange Date Crumbles: Substitute orange juice for the water in the filling and add the zest of a medium orange. **Cocoa Date Crumbles**: Add 4 tbsp cocoa to the filling.

Hazelnut or Almond Date Crumbles: Prepare filling as usual. Add ½ cup ground almonds or hazelnuts plus 1 tsp cinnamon and ½ tsp nutmeg to the crumble.

Winter Whites

PREP TIME: **20** MINUTES + CHILLING TIME | COOK TIME: **10** MINUTES | MAKES **2½** TO **3** DOZEN

I had to ask my mom and her twin sister where this cookie-bar recipe came from because we've been making them for so long in our family: for forty years at least. My mother confirmed my suspicion that the recipe came into our hands via an old local church cookbook. We all still make them for the Christmas freezer every year, and there's no doubt they'll be made in our family for many years more, especially since they're a favourite among our kids and their cousins too. While the filling is cooked on the stove, it's strictly a no-bake recipe, so it's something you can easily accomplish while you have another batch of Christmas goodies in the oven.

graham crackers to line the bottom of the pan

¾ cup melted butter

¾ cup sugar

1½ tsp vanilla extract

3 beaten eggs

3 cups graham cracker crumbs

1 cup fine dried coconut

2½ cups mini marshmallow

1½ cups whipped cream (or use a whipped topping substitute)

1 tsp vanilla extract

4 tbsp icing sugar (powdered sugar)

VANILLA FROSTING (OPTIONAL)
2 cups icing sugar (powdered sugar)

½ cup butter

1 tsp vanilla extract

1–2 tbsp milk

1. Lightly grease and line the bottom and sides of a 9x13-inch baking pan with parchment paper.

2. Line the bottom of the pan with graham crackers. Cut as needed to fit.

3. In a medium saucepan over medium-low heat, combine the melted butter, sugar, and 1½ tsp vanilla extract.

4. Cook for only a couple of minutes, stirring constantly until hot and the sugar is dissolved.

5. Quickly whisk in the beaten eggs.

6. Cook for only about a minute before removing from the heat and very quickly stirring in the graham crumbs and coconut.

7. Let it cool for a minute before folding in the mini marshmallows.

8. Spread the prepared mixture evenly over the crackers and chill well for a couple of hours or overnight.

9. Beat together the whipping cream, 1 tsp vanilla extract, and powdered sugar until stiff peaks form.

10. Top the chilled cookie bars with whipped cream, cut in squares and serve. These freeze very well, but you might like to use a non-dairy whipped topping to freeze them with the cream already on them. If not, freeze them without the whipped cream and just add it before serving.

Alternatively, you could make a simple vanilla frosting for the top before cutting and freezing them.

VANILLA FROSTING (OPTIONAL)

1. Beat together the butter, icing sugar, vanilla, and milk until light, fluffy, and of a good spreadable consistency.

2. Add the milk only a little at a time until the proper consistency is achieved.

Apricot Almond Jammie Dodgers

PREP TIME: **30** MINUTES + CHILLING TIME | COOK TIME: **30** MINUTES | MAKES ABOUT **3** DOZEN

2 cups **flour**

1 cup **icing sugar** (powdered sugar)

pinch **salt**

½ cup finely **ground almonds**

1 cup + 2 tbsp **cold butter**, cut in cubes

3 large **egg yolks**

2 tsp **vanilla extract**

½ tsp **almond extract**

12-14 rounded tsp **homemade** or **good quality apricot jam**

This is a terrific recipe to make with the kids, allowing them to choose their favourite cookie-cutter shapes and cutting the cookies out themselves. They may not be too fond of apricot, but luckily any good quality jam can be substituted. I also have it on good authority that in the United Kingdom, Father Christmas loves Jammie Dodgers, so be sure to have the kids leave some out for him too.

Regular readers of my blog will know two things about me for sure. One is that I love all things apricot, and the second is that I love British baking. This recipe allowed me to indulge both of those passions at once while making a very pretty addition to my repertoire of Christmas cookies.

1. Sift together the flour, icing sugar, salt, and ground almonds. Set aside.

2. Rub the butter into the dry ingredients with your fingers until well incorporated and the mixture becomes crumbly, like a coarse meal.

3. Whisk together the egg yolks, vanilla, and almond extracts. Add to the crumbly dry mixture and mix in until a soft dough forms.

4. Wrap the dough in plastic wrap and chill in the fridge for at least 30 minutes.

5. Preheat oven to 350°F. Roll the dough out between two pieces of lightly floured parchment paper to about ⅛ of an inch thick.

6. Cut out cookies using a 3-inch cutter and place on a parchment-lined baking sheet. Cut circles or hearts or whatever shape you like out of the centers of half of the cookies.

7. Bake for 15-20 minutes, just until they start to brown slightly at the bottom edges but are still very pale.

8. Remove from the oven and spoon 1 rounded teaspoon of apricot jam (or your favourite jam) onto the middle of the bottom halves of the cookies and spread out only slightly to about ¾ of an inch from the edge of the cookie. Carefully lay the top halves of the cookies onto the jam and press down lightly.

9. Return to the oven for an additional 5-6 minutes. This will heat up the jam to a point where it will stick the two cookie halves together.

10. Cool on the baking sheet for 10 minutes before transferring the cookies to a wire rack to cool completely. Store in airtight containers.

Chocolate Arrowroot Cookie Squares

PREP TIME: **20** MINUTES | COOK TIME: **5** MINUTES | MAKES ABOUT **3** DOZEN SQUARES

ARROWROOT COOKIE BASE

28 Arrowroot cookies

5 tbsp cocoa

7 tbsp sugar

⅓ cup melted butter

1 tsp vanilla extract

pinch salt

3 beaten eggs

CHOCOLATE MIDDLE LAYER

½ cup unsalted butter

4 tbsp cocoa

4 tbsp sugar

3 tbsp flour

3 tbsp boiling water

3 tbsp milk

pinch salt

VANILLA WHIPPED CREAM

1 cup whipping cream

3 tbsp icing sugar (powdered sugar)

1 tsp vanilla extract

As a child, I first remember these simple and delicious no-bake cookie squares as being made by Aunt Marion Morgan from Port-de-Grave, my mother's hometown. She was an "aunt" in the Newfoundland sense of the word, where the "aunt" and "uncle" were more commonly used as terms of respect for your elders than as a reference to a blood relative. Though Aunt Marion had no children of her own, she welcomed the seemingly endless rabble of grandchildren visiting my grandparents a couple of doors up the lane. We were always hopeful on those visits that she had made some of her famous Arrowroot Squares. She's still remembered every year at Christmas when many of those kids in our family now make them as a favourite holiday treat for their own children.

1. For the base, first break up the Arrowroot cookies into small pieces about the size of a postage stamp or smaller.

2. In a medium saucepan, combine the cocoa, sugar, melted butter, vanilla, salt, and beaten eggs.

3. Place on medium-low heat and cook, scraping the bottom of the pot constantly until the mixture resembles soft scrambled eggs. You want to make sure the eggs are thoroughly cooked but not completely dried out.

4. Add the broken Arrowroot cookies, mix well to combine together, and press into the bottom of a greased or parchment-lined 9x9-inch baking dish.

5. Set in fridge to cool for about 20 minutes.

6. While the base is cooling, mix together all of the ingredients for the chocolate middle layer. Beat together very well until smooth and fluffy and spread evenly over the prepared base.

7.   If serving these right away, you can top them with Vanilla Whipped Cream and chocolate shavings. If you plan on freezing these, use a commercial brand non-dairy whipped topping because it holds up better to freezing.

VANILLA WHIPPED CREAM

1.   Combine the whipping cream, icing sugar, and vanilla in a small bowl and whip to firm peaks.

Strawberry Chiffon Squares

PREP TIME: **15** MINUTES + SETTING TIME | MAKES ABOUT **36** SQUARES

This is a very old recipe that I first remember being made by my mom's twin sister, Muriel, but it's been adopted by almost everyone in our extended family as a regular Christmas treat. Although I don't think the original recipe called for them to be frozen, that is the way they have come to be enjoyed in our family. They freeze to an almost ice-cream-like consistency, which makes them ideal to pull from the freezer for a quick dessert at any time during the holiday season.

GRAHAM CRUMB BASE

¾ cup melted butter

4 tbsp white sugar

3 cups graham cracker crumbs

STRAWBERRY CHIFFON TOP LAYER

¾ cup boiling water

2 small pkgs strawberry Jell-O

1 can sweetened condensed milk

¼ cup lemon juice

one 16 oz tub frozen strawberries in syrup, chopped small

8 oz (250 g) mini marshmallows

16 oz whipped cream, beaten to stiff peaks

GRAHAM CRUMB BASE

1. Mix together the butter, sugar, and graham cracker crumbs.

2. Lightly grease and line a 9x13-inch baking pan with parchment paper.

3. Press the crumb mixture evenly into the prepared pan.

STRAWBERRY CHIFFON TOP LAYER

1. Combine the boiling water and Jell-O, stir until dissolved.

2. Add sweetened milk, lemon juice, and strawberries, including the syrup.

3. Fold in marshmallows and whipped cream.

4. Spread over prepared base and chill until the Jell-O has set.

5. These can also be served frozen; in fact many people prefer them frozen and that's almost always how I serve them. They defrost pretty quickly, so I always store these in the freezer anyway.

This dessert takes very little time to prepare but is best made in advance to allow the Jell-O to set or even the day before if serving as a frozen dessert. This is a very old recipe, and I'm told that in many places the frozen tubs of strawberries in syrup are no longer available. Not to worry. Here's how to make a substitute:

1 lb **fresh strawberries**

¼ cup **water**

½ cup **sugar**

Simply clean and hull the strawberries and dice them small. Add them to a small saucepan with the water and sugar and bring to a boil for only 1 minute. Turn off the heat and let the mixture cool to room temperature or cooler. This should produce about 2 cups of strawberries in syrup as needed in the recipe.

Chocolate Mint Nanaimo Bars

PREP TIME: **15** MINUTES + CHILLING TIME | MAKES **24** COOKIE BARS

BASE LAYER

½ cup butter

¼ cup sugar

5 tbsp cocoa

1 beaten egg

1¾ cups graham cracker crumbs

¾ cup fine or medium unsweetened coconut

½ cup finely chopped walnuts

MINT FROSTING FILLING

½ cup butter

2 tsp pure mint extract

2 cups icing sugar (powdered sugar)

CHOCOLATE TOPPING

1 cup chocolate chips

2 tbsp butter

½ tsp pure mint extract

There are many chocolate-mint lovers out there, especially at Christmas time when the flavour combination seems to get even more popular. Canada is also an entire nation of Nanaimo Bar lovers, so the marriage of these two delicious concepts is a natural. While perfect for the Christmas freezer, a Nanaimo Bar of any description is going to be a year-round favourite. Serve these on a mixed platter of homemade cookies and see which ones disappear first.

BASE LAYER

1. Melt together the butter, sugar, and cocoa over low heat.

2. Add the egg, continue to cook, stirring constantly to fully cook the egg to a soft scrambled texture.

3. Add the graham crumbs, coconut, and walnuts.

4. Mix together until well combined then press into the bottom of a parchment-lined 9x9-inch baking pan.

MINT FROSTING FILLING

1. With an electric mixer, beat together the butter, mint extract, and icing sugar until smooth.

2. This frosting should be very stiff but spreadable (much thicker than you would use to frost a cake, for example). If you think it's too thick, you may add a few drops of milk at a time to bring it to the right consistency.

3. Spread evenly over the bottom layer. Chill in the fridge for a couple of hours before adding the chocolate topping.

CHOCOLATE TOPPING

1. Melt together the chocolate chips, mint extract, and butter over low heat, just until the chocolate is just melted—don't over heat it.

2. Spread quickly over the chilled frosted layer. Return to the fridge until the chocolate sets. Cut into squares or bars. These cookie bars freeze very well.

Cherry Vanilla Cheesecake Bars

PREP TIME: **20** MINUTES | COOK TIME: **35** MINUTES | MAKES ABOUT **16** COOKIE BARS

1½ cups flour

⅓ cup firmly packed brown sugar

½ cup cold butter

1 cup (8 oz) cream cheese

½ cup white sugar

3 tsp vanilla extract

1 tbsp lemon juice

1 large egg

⅔ cup glacé cherries, cut in quarters (well-drained maraschino cherries will also work. I rinse them and drain them on paper towels before cutting them)

These cheesecake bars are one of the most popular posts ever on *RockRecipes.com*, and they always see a surge of hits around the Christmas season. Maybe it's because they turn out so pretty or that they are so easy to prepare, even for a beginner, or that they are a great way to portion control for cheesecake lovers, or that they freeze well for later, or...well, it starts to become obvious why they are so popular, doesn't it?

1. Preheat oven to 350°F.

2. In a food processor, pulse together the flour, brown sugar, and butter until crumbly (or simply cut the butter through the flour and sugar with a pastry knife or two butter knives held between your fingers).

3. Save ½ cup of this crumble mixture to sprinkle over the top later.

4. Press the rest of the crumble mixture into the bottom of a greased or parchment-lined 8x8-inch baking pan.

5. Bake for 15 minutes. Remove from oven and let cool for a few minutes while preparing the cheesecake filling. Reduce the oven temperature to 325°F.

6. Beat together the cream cheese, white sugar, lemon juice, and vanilla extract until smooth.

7. Beat in the egg and then fold in the chopped cherries.

8. Spread the cheesecake mixture evenly onto the pre-baked cookie base and sprinkle the reserved cookie crumble over the surface.

9. Bake for 20-30 minutes or until the cheesecake is set at the center.

10. Let cool completely in the pan before cutting and serving. Refrigerate in airtight containers. Freezes well too.

Apricot Coconut Cookie Bars

PREP TIME: **30** MINUTES | COOK TIME: **45** MINUTES | MAKES ABOUT **36** COOKIE BARS

These cookie bars were inspired by a lemon version of this recipe that has been a favourite in my family for decades. My mother and I both love anything with apricots and coconut, so I decided one Christmas to make this version of the family favourite. I always thought people who liked the flavour of apricots were in the minority, but this recipe was an instant hit with *Rock Recipes* followers. Make a batch for your Christmas freezer and I'll bet you'll discover a lot of apricot loving friends and family over the holidays.

APRICOT FILLING

3 cups dried apricots, chopped fine

1 cup sugar

1½ cups boiling water

COCONUT COOKIE BARS

2 cups flour

¾ cup sugar

1 tsp baking powder

2 cups dried coconut, medium cut

pinch salt

1 cup butter, cut in small pieces

APRICOT FILLING

1.   Simmer the chopped apricots in the sugar and water until the apricots are softened and the mixture comes to a jam-like consistency.

2.   Alternatively, you can use a good quality apricot jam. You will need about 2½ cups.

COCONUT COOKIE BARS

1.   Preheat oven to 350°F.

2.   Sift together the flour, sugar, baking powder, coconut, and salt.

3.   Using your hands or a pastry blender, cut the butter into the dry ingredients until it is completely incorporated and the mixture resembles a coarse crumbly meal.

4.   Press half of the crumb mixture into the bottom of a 9x13-inch well-greased baking pan.

5.   Pour the apricot filling evenly over the bottom crumbs. Gently sprinkle the remaining crumbs over the apricot filling and press down gently.

6.   Bake for 40-45 minutes or until light golden brown in colour. Cool completely in the pan before cutting into squares and serving.

APRICOT FRUITCAKE

CAKES

Cherry Pound Cake

PREP TIME: **30** MINUTES | COOK TIME: **60** MINUTES | MAKES **1** LARGE CAKE OR **2** SMALLER LOAVES

Here in Newfoundland, a cherry cake is an absolute must for Christmas. A moist, dense pound cake with glacé cherries and flavoured with almond extract, this treat is a universal Christmas favourite in almost every Newfoundland household I know. This recipe came from a family friend decades ago, and it's the one I've been using ever since because of the added richness and flavour provided by using undiluted evaporated milk in the batter. Cherry cake is also great for gift giving at Christmas time, and we regularly make many of these as loaf cakes for friends and neighbours every year.

1 lb chopped **glacé cherries** +
¼ cup **flour**

1½ cups **butter**

2 cups **sugar**

3 **eggs**

2 tsp **vanilla extract**

2 tsp **almond extract**

3 cups **flour**

1½ tsp **baking powder**

1 cup lukewarm, undiluted
evaporated milk

Baking times vary greatly on this recipe, so rely on the toothpick test to ensure it is properly baked. When a wooden toothpick inserted in the center comes out clean, it's done. Be careful not to go past this stage or the cake will be dry.

1. Preheat oven to 325°F.

2. Rinse the cherries in a colander to remove any syrup they may have been stored in. Pat them dry between layers of paper towels. This step helps prevent the cherries sinking into the batter as well. Depending on their size, cut them into halves or quarters and set aside for later. They will get tossed in ¼ cup of flour later but not until just before they are folded into the batter.

3. Cream together the butter and sugar well.

4. Add the eggs, one at a time, beating well after each addition until light and fluffy.

5. Beat in the vanilla and almond extracts.

6. Sift together the 3 cups of flour and baking powder.

7. Fold dry ingredients into the creamed mixture alternately with the lukewarm milk, beginning and ending with the dry ingredients. As a general rule, I add the dry ingredients in 3 portions and the milk in 2 portions.

8. Fold in the chopped cherries that have been tossed at the last minute in the ¼ cup flour.

9. Bake in a greased and floured springform pan, tube pan, or 2 loaf pans, lined with parchment paper. Bake for 45-60 minutes, depending on the size of your pan.

10. Let the cake cool in the pan(s) for 10 minutes before turning out onto a wire rack to cool completely.

English Style Dark Fruitcake

PREP TIME: **45** MINUTES | COOK TIME: **1½** TO **2** HOURS | MAKES **1** LARGE CAKE

¾ cup **butter**

6 oz **dried prunes**, chopped

6 oz **dates**, chopped

8 oz **dark raisins**

6 oz **golden raisins**

6 oz **currents**

1 cup **dark brown sugar**

¾ cup **molasses**

2 tsp **allspice**

2 tsp **cinnamon**

2 tsp **powdered ginger**

1 tsp **cloves**

2 tsp **nutmeg**

½ cup **coffee liqueur** (or ½ cup strong black coffee)

zest and juice of 2 oranges

3 **eggs**, beaten

1⅓ cups **all-purpose flour**

3 tbsp **cocoa**

½ tsp **baking powder**

½ tsp **baking soda**

½ cup **ground hazelnuts or almonds**

8 oz **glacé cherries**

8 oz **candied citrus peel**

8 oz **toasted pecans**, roughly chopped

4 oz **dark rum** (or your favorite whiskey or brandy)

There's just no doubt about it—you either like fruitcake or you don't. I've loved it since I was a small child, particularly a dark, molasses and spice flavoured fruitcake like this one. Spouse is equally, if not more of a fan than me! The scent of baking fruitcake is the smell of Christmas to both of us. It's something we look forward to every year.

This recipe was tweaked and refined over the years and now stands as my ideal example of the perfect dark fruitcake: rich, dense, moist, and well spiced. It has been a tradition in our house for over twenty years. This is a large cake that's meant to be served in small pieces. There are easily forty portions or more.

1.   Grease a 10-inch springform pan, a large tube pan, or two 9x5-inch loaf pans and line with parchment paper.

2.   In a large saucepan, melt the butter over medium heat and add the prunes, dates, raisins, currents, brown sugar, molasses, spices, coffee liqueur (or coffee), and the orange zest and juice.

3.   Bring to a gentle boil and very slowly simmer for 10 minutes.

4.   Remove from heat and allow to cool for 30-45 minutes.

5.   Preheat oven to 300°F.

6.   When cool, stir in the beaten eggs.

7.   Sift together flour, cocoa, baking powder, and baking soda.

8.   Add the ground nuts and fold through the boiled mixture.

9.   Fold in cherries, citrus peel, and pecans. Pour into prepared baking pan. You can decorate the top with additional pecan halves, cherries, etc., if you like.

10. Bake for 1½ to 2 hours, depending on the size of your pan. Mine took the full 2 hours in a 10-inch springform pan. Loaf

pans would take less time, 1-1 ¼ hours. The cake should feel firm to the touch at the center, and a wooden toothpick inserted into the center should come out clean. If that takes a little longer than the estimated time, don't worry, this recipe is pretty forgiving. The cake should be cooled completely in the pan on a wire rack before removing.

11. At this point, you can poke small holes in the top and bottom of the cake with a fork and pour on the dark rum. Pour half on the top, wait ten minutes, then flip it over and pour the remaining half on the bottom.

12. Soak several layers of cheesecloth in additional rum if you like and wrap completely around the cake, then cover with several layers of plastic wrap and store in a COOL place for up to several weeks before Christmas.

13. When serving, you can add a layer of marzipan or if you have decorated the top with fruit and nuts, brush with a simple glaze of equal parts water and sugar boiled together for about 10-15 minutes.

Apricot Raisin Cake *and* Apricot Fruitcake

PREP TIME: **30** MINUTES + STANDING TIME | COOK TIME: **1** HOUR **30** MINUTES

MAKES **1** BUNDT-SIZED CAKE OR **2** SMALL LOAF CAKES

FRUIT MIXTURE

2 cups **water**

¼ cup **sugar**

12 oz dried chopped **apricots**

½ cup **sultana raisins**

CAKE BATTER

1 cup **butter**

1 cup **sugar**

1½ tsp **vanilla extract**

4 oz **cream cheese**

4 **eggs**

2½ cups **flour**

1 tsp **baking powder**

> ❄
>
> To make this cake as an
> **Apricot Fruitcake**,
> simply add the following
> ingredients to the apricot
> raisin mixture after it has
> completely cooled: 1 lb
> **glacé cherries**, chopped
> and 1 lb **mixed fruit**.
> (See photo on page 48)

This is another recipe that has become popularized in Newfoundland baking in the last couple of decades or so. I know people from several different parts of the province who make a version of this apricot raisin cake at Christmas time and other special occasions. One friend even chose it as her wedding cake. The cream cheese enriched batter and very moist texture account for its popularity. A couple of years ago I added some additional glacé fruits to this recipe and created a simple fruitcake version that has been a hit on *RockRecipes.com* every Christmas since.

FRUIT MIXTURE

1.   It is generally best to make the fruit mixture a day ahead and let it stand overnight to absorb the maximum amount of liquid.

2.   In a medium saucepan, combine the water, sugar, apricots, and raisins.

3.   Simmer very gently for 30 minutes or until there is almost no liquid left. Cool completely.

CAKE BATTER

1.   Preheat oven to 350°F.

2.   Cream the butter, sugar, vanilla extract, and cream cheese until light and fluffy.

3.   Add the eggs, one at a time, beating well after each addition.

4.   Sift together the flour and baking powder.

5.   Fold half of the dry ingredients into the creamed mixture.

6.   Fold in the apricot mixture, followed by the remaining dry ingredients.

7. Bake in a greased and floured tube pan or two small greased loaf pans for about 60 minutes or until a toothpick inserted in the center comes out clean.

8. Baking times may vary on this recipe depending on the amount of moisture contained in the boiled fruit mixture. The toothpick test is the best way to determine when it is done.

Poor Man's Cake (War Cake)

PREP TIME: **20** MINUTES + COOLING TIME | COOK TIME: **60** MINUTES | SERVES **16**

One year in particular, in the weeks before Christmas, I began getting requests for a War Cake recipe, and at first I replied I'd never heard of it. But in fact, our family has been making it for decades. Said to be a recipe adapted to the limited available ingredients due to rationing during World War II, we know this cake in our family as Poor Man's Cake, and my mom's recipe for it is absolutely delicious. By either name, this is one delicious, moist raisin spice cake, and although it's made without eggs or milk, you would never know it. It stays moist for days in a covered container, but you may want to try it warm out of the oven with some rum and butter sauce for a terrific dessert at any time during the holidays.

---

2 cups **raisins**

3 cups **water**

1½ cups **sugar**

½ cup **butter**

3 cups **flour**

1 tsp **baking powder**

1 tsp **baking soda**

½ tsp **ground ginger**

½ tsp **cloves**

½ tsp **nutmeg**

1 tsp **cinnamon**

1.   In a small saucepan, combine the raisins and water. Bring to a rolling boil and continue to boil for about 10 minutes.

2.   Remove from the heat and stir in the sugar and butter.

3.   Stir until the butter is melted and the sugar is dissolved. This step can be done a day in advance if you prefer. Let this mixture cool for at least a couple of hours until it reaches room temperature.

4.   Preheat the oven to 350°F.

5.   Sift together the flour, baking powder, baking soda, and spices.

6.   Pour the raisin mixture onto the dry ingredients and stir with a wooden spoon until well blended but do not overmix the batter. Pour the batter into a well-greased and floured Bundt pan or tube pan.

7.   Bake for about 60 minutes or until a toothpick inserted in the center comes out clean.

8.   Cool in the pan for 10 minutes before turning the cake out onto a wire rack to cool completely. Store in an airtight container or cake tin.

9. Baking times vary greatly on this recipe, so rely on the toothpick test to ensure it is properly baked. When a wooden toothpick inserted in the center comes out clean, it's done. Be careful not to go past this stage or the cake will be dry.

10. Let the cake cool in the pan(s) for an hour before transferring it, right side up, to a wire rack to cool completely.

11. At this point, when cooled, you can poke small holes in the top and bottom of the cake with a fork and pour on 4–8 oz of light rum, coconut rum, or brandy; half on the top, wait ten minutes, then flip it over and pour the remaining half on the bottom.

12. Soak several layers of cheesecloth in additional rum or brandy if you like and wrap completely around the cake, then cover with several layers of plastic wrap and store in a COOL place for a couple of weeks at least.

BREADS
AND DESSERT

Lassie Raisin Bread

PREP TIME: **30** MINUTES + RISING TIME | COOK TIME: **40** TO **50** MINUTES | MAKES **4** LOAVES

2 tbsp white sugar

1 cup lukewarm water

2 tsp or two 8g envelopes dry yeast

8 cups (approx.) all-purpose flour

1 tsp salt

¾ cup melted butter

1 cup molasses

1½ cups lukewarm milk

2 beaten eggs

3 cups raisins

In the last few remaining baking days leading up to Christmas, I like to make this incredibly popular Newfoundland Molasses Raisin Bread commonly referred to in this province as "Lassie Raisin Bread." This is another of those iconic Newfoundland recipes that every native Newfoundlander's mother or grandmother used to make and hopefully still does.

This bread is fantastic warm, straight out of the oven with gobs of melting butter, but it also makes the absolute best toast ever! Molasses raisin toast is a bit of a Christmas Eve or Christmas morning tradition in our house. I normally make several loaves for the freezer too and a few extra loaves for a couple of lucky gift recipients. Anyone who gets one of these loaves is in for a real treat.

1.   In a small bowl, stir the sugar into the lukewarm water and then sprinkle the yeast over the top. Let stand without stirring for 10 minutes.

2.   In a large mixing bowl or the bowl of an electric mixer that has a dough hook, stir together 3 cups of the flour along with the salt. When the yeast is ready, stir it and add it to the flour and salt along with the butter, molasses, warm milk, and beaten eggs.

3.   Using a wooden spoon or the regular paddle of your electric mixer, mix slowly for 4-5 minutes until the mixture is smooth with no lumps. If using an electric mixer, switch to the dough hook at this point and begin to slowly incorporate the remaining flour. You may need to use a little more or less flour than the recipe details to bring your dough to a proper consistency that is not too sticky. This is not unusual.

4.   If not using an electric mixer, keep mixing in the flour gradually until a soft dough forms that leaves the sides of the bowl.

5.   Add the raisins at this point and continue to knead until the raisins are evenly distributed in the dough.

6.   Turn the dough out onto a flour-dusted countertop or breadboard to knead. Knead the dough for an additional 5-10 minutes by hand.

7.   Place the dough in a large bowl and cover with a damp tea towel. Leave it to rest and rise for 2

hours. Punch the dough down and knead it for a few minutes by hand before letting it rest for another 10 minutes.

8. Grease 4 medium loaf pans, 9x5 inches at the top or similar dimensions. Divide the dough into 12 equal portions. Form each portion into a ball. I use a kitchen scale for this purpose, taking the total weight of the dough and then dividing by 12.

9. Place 3 balls of dough in each prepared loaf pan. Cover with a clean tea towel and allow the dough to rise until it is about 2 inches above the rim of the pan, about 2-3 hours depending on room temperature. Molasses bread generally takes quite a bit longer to rise/proof than white bread.

10. Preheat oven to 350°F and bake for 40-50 minutes depending on the size of the pans you are using. The top and bottom crust should have good colour.

11. When baked, turn the loaves out onto a wire rack to cool. Brush the tops with melted butter, if desired, to soften the top crust.

Fruit Bread

I like to think of this as a versatile base recipe that can be changed to suit your taste. I've used different kinds of dried glacé fruits, candied mixed citrus peel, and even just plain glacé cherries in this beautiful breakfast bread over the years. The mixed fruit version is still my favourite, but even then I'll add a few extra cherries into the mix, especially if I have red and green on hand, to make it look just that little bit more festive: perfect for a fresh-from-the-oven Christmas Eve treat and then for toast on Christmas morning.

8 cups (approx.) **flour**

½ cup **sugar**

1 pkg **instant yeast**

1 tsp **salt**

½ cup **melted butter**

2 cups **warm milk**

2 **eggs**

2 tsp **vanilla extract**

1½ cups **mixed glacé fruit**

1 cup **glacé cherries**, quartered

1. Combine 3 cups of the flour along with the sugar, instant yeast, and salt in a large bowl or in the bowl of a large electric mixer that uses a dough hook.

2. Add the melted butter, warm milk, eggs, and vanilla extract.

3. Using a wooden spoon or the regular paddle of your electric mixer, mix for 4-5 minutes at slow speed until the mixture is smooth with no lumps.

4. If using an electric mixer, switch to the dough hook at this point and begin to slowly incorporate the remaining flour. If not using an electric mixer, keep mixing in the flour gradually until a soft dough forms that leaves the sides of the bowl. You may need to use a little less or a little more flour than indicated in the recipe, this is not uncommon.

5. Knead the dough for an additional 10 minutes either in the electric mixer or on a floured breadboard or countertop.

6. Place dough in a large bowl and leave to rest and let it rise for only about 45 minutes.

7. Punch the dough down and gently knead in the glacé cherries by hand for a few minutes just enough to distribute them evenly throughout the dough.

8. Grease 3 large or 4 medium loaf pans. Medium pans measure 9x5 inches across the top. Divide dough in 3 or 4 equal portions and form into loaves.

9. Place 1 ball of dough in each greased loaf pan to rise. Cover with a clean tea towel and let rise until about triple in size, rising about 1-2 inches above the pan: about 2 hours.

10. Preheat oven to 350°F and bake for about 35-40 minutes or until golden brown and a good bottom crust has formed (about 45-50 minutes for larger loaves).

11. Brush the tops of the loaves with butter or honey if desired, while they are still warm.

❄

The dough from one of the loaves can be used to make **Christmas Hot Cross Buns**. Just divide the dough into 12 equal balls, let them rise until doubled in size, and bake in a greased 9x13-inch pan for about 25-30 minutes at 350°F. Use 1 cup of icing sugar mixed with a tablespoon or two of milk to make a glaze to pipe crosses onto the cooled buns.

Christmas Chelsea Buns

PREP TIME: **30** MINUTES + RISING TIME | COOK TIME: **30** TO **35** MINUTES | MAKES **12** LARGE BUNS

DOUGH

3 cups **all-purpose flour**

¼ cup **sugar**

1 tsp (envelope) **instant dry yeast**

¼ tsp **salt**

¼ cup **melted butter**

1¼ cups **warm milk**

1 tsp **vanilla extract**

2 **eggs**, slightly beaten

FILLING

½ cup **brown sugar**

½ cup **soft butter**

1½ tsp **cinnamon**

1 tsp **nutmeg**

¼ tsp **cloves**

zest of 1 **orange**, finely grated

1 cup **mixed glacé fruit**

½ cup chopped **glacé cherries**

½ cup **currents**

GLAZE

½ cup **apricot jam**

1–2 tbsp **water**

One of the things I love about Christmas these days is the annual crop of new Christmas cooking and baking specials on TV and online, especially those coming out of the UK. So many of our Christmas traditions in this country come from those found in our English, Irish, Scottish, and Welsh roots. Although Chelsea buns are popular year round in the UK, I make them just a little more festive at Christmas time with the addition of a little spice and the fragrant zest of an orange mixed into the fruit filling. Try them and they may just become a new Christmas tradition in your family.

1. Combine 2 cups of the flour along with the sugar, instant yeast, and salt in a large bowl or in the bowl of a large electric mixer that uses a dough hook.

2. Add the melted butter, warm milk, vanilla extract, and eggs.

3. Using a wooden spoon or the regular paddle of your electric mixer, mix slowly for 4-5 minutes until the mixture is smooth with no lumps.

4. If using an electric mixer, switch to the dough hook at this point and begin to slowly incorporate the remaining 1 cup of flour. If not using an electric mixer, keep mixing in the flour gradually until a soft dough forms that leaves the sides of the bowl. You may need to use a little less or a little more flour, this is not uncommon.

5. Knead the dough for an additional 10 minutes either in the electric mixer or on a breadboard or countertop.

6. Cover dough and leave to rest and rise for 60 minutes. Punch the dough down and knead it for a few minutes by hand before letting it rest for another 10 minutes.

7. Roll the rested dough out into a large rectangle about 12x18 inches.

8. Mix all of the ingredients for the filling together and spread as evenly as possible over the rolled dough.

9. Starting at the short side of the rectangle, roll the dough into a log, pinching the dough together to seal at the end of the roll.

10. Cut the roll into 12 equal slices, and place on a parchment-lined cookie sheet.

11. Cover the baking sheet with a clean tea towel and allow the rolls to rise until at least doubled in size, about 1 to 1½ hours. (I sometimes let them rise in the fridge overnight and pop them into the oven in the morning. I've also frozen them before they rise and take them out of the freezer to rise overnight on the countertop before going to bed.)

12. Preheat oven to 350°F and bake for 30-40 minutes or until the rolls are well browned and spring back when touched in the center.

13. To add an optional glaze to the buns, microwave the apricot jam with a tablespoon or 2 of water until it is hot and pourable. Brush on while the buns are still hot. You can also use a little honey to glaze if you prefer.

Butter Tarts

PREP TIME: **45** MINUTES | COOK TIME: **15** MINUTES | MAKES ABOUT **12** TARTS

While I absolutely adore butter tarts, they are not part of the Christmas baking tradition in my family. But every Christmas at *RockRecipes.com*, the hits for this butter-tart recipe skyrocket. People from all across Canada definitely enjoy them as a long-time part of their holiday traditions, and I've heard from many who tell of their mothers and grandmothers lovingly preparing them each year.

PASTRY

½ cup **shortening**, very cold and cut in cubes

½ cup **butter**, very cold and cut in cubes

2¼ cups **flour** (pastry flour is best to use but all–purpose will do)

1 tbsp **brown sugar**

½ tsp **salt**

6 tbsp **ice water** (enough to bring the dough together)

FILLING

½ cup lightly packed **brown sugar**

½ cup **corn syrup**

¼ cup **melted butter**

1 **egg**

1 tsp **vanilla extract**

¼ tsp **salt**

½ cup **raisins** (substituting pecans, walnuts, or chocolate chips also makes good variations)

PASTRY

1. Pulse the cold butter and shortening into the flour, sugar, and salt using a food processor until the shortening or butter is reduced to pea-sized pieces.

2. Sprinkle the water over the surface and toss with a fork until the water is just incorporated into the dough. Do not over work the dough; handle it only enough so the dough stays together.

3. Form the dough into two rounds about 1 inch thick.

4. Wrap in plastic wrap and let rest in the fridge for about 30 minutes.

5. Roll out on lightly floured surface. Cut into rounds with a 4-inch cutter. Fit into muffin cups. Chill in the fridge or freezer while you prepare the filling. Cold pastry heading into a hot oven will always be flakier.

FILLING

1. Preheat oven to 425°F.

2. Combine all filling ingredients except raisins.

3. Mix well.

4. Sprinkle raisins in a single layer in the bottom of the pastry-lined muffin cups.

5. Fill ⅔ full with syrup mixture.

6. Bake on bottom shelf of oven for 12-15 minutes.

7. Cool completely on a wire rack and remove tarts from pans.

 There is considerable debate about whether the filling in a butter tart should be runny or firm. Preferences vary, especially geographically, but if you want a firmer, less runny filling, simply add an additional egg, increase the brown sugar to ¾ cup, and decrease the corn syrup to ¼ cup.

Figgy Pudding *with* Rum and Butter Sauce

PREP TIME: **30** MINUTES | COOK TIME: **2** HOURS | SERVES UP TO **8**

FIGGY PUDDING

1 cup **dates**, chopped

¾ cup chopped **dried figs**

¼ cup **golden raisins**

½ cup **mixed glacé fruit**

¼ cup **currents**

1½ cups **water**

zest of ½ a large **orange**

¼ cup **dark rum**

⅓ cup **butter**

⅓ cup **molasses**

1 cup firmly packed **brown sugar**

2 tsp **vanilla extract**

2 large **eggs**

1⅔ cups **flour**

1 tsp **baking powder**

1 tsp **baking soda**

1½ tsp **cinnamon**

¼ tsp **ground cloves**

RUM AND BUTTER SAUCE

½ cup **salted butter**

1 cup **brown sugar**

¼ cup **amber or dark rum**

1 tsp **vanilla extract**

1 cup **whipping cream**

With yet another nod to our British culinary traditions, this pudding has become a more recent addition to our family's Christmas table in an attempt at resurrecting an old-fashioned favourite. What could be Christmassier than a figgy pudding? Or more delicious? This one has a texture much like another British favourite, Sticky Toffee Pudding, with the added fragrance of spices and orange zest. Serve it with this amazing rum and butter sauce for one of the richest, most indulgent desserts of the season. You'll wonder why we ever abandoned this delicious tradition at all.

FIGGY PUDDING

1. Add the dates, figs, raisins, mixed fruit, currents, and water to a small saucepan. Simmer slowly for 15 minutes or so until all of the water has been absorbed and the mixture is paste-like. Allow this mixture to cool completely before stirring in the orange zest and rum.

2. Prepare your steamer by greasing it well and lightly dusting with flour. You will need a 7-cup or larger steamer for this pudding. I sometimes use a heat-proof Pyrex bowl covered tightly in plastic wrap with an outside layer of aluminum foil. I've also used a Bundt pan many times as a steamer. The only caution there is to make sure the hole in the center is completely plugged or the pudding will get wet. A wine cork of the right size, or some balled-up plastic wrap stuffed in the hole will work well for this purpose. Again, the top should be covered tightly with plastic wrap and then a layer of aluminum foil before placing it into the boiling water. The pot that you place your steamer in should be about 1½ times the size of the steamer and should have a metal trivet on the bottom. Do not let your pudding steamer touch the bottom of the pot. An old stoneware tea plate can make an adequate trivet if necessary. Bring about 2 inches of water to a slow simmer in the pot to get it ready.

3. Cream the butter, molasses, and brown sugar well before blending in the vanilla extract.

4. Beat in the eggs, one at a time, beating well after each addition. Stir the cooled date and fig mixture through the creamed mixture.

5. Finally, sift together the flour, baking powder, baking soda, cinnamon, cloves, and nutmeg. Fold the dry ingredients into the mixture until well incorporated. Spread the batter evenly into the prepared steamer. Add the cover to the steamer (or a layer each of plastic wrap then aluminum foil to stop water seeping in).

6. Place the steamer on the trivet at the bottom of the boiling water and place the lid on the pot.

7. Steam the pudding for 2 hours. Test it to see if a wooden toothpick inserted in the center comes out clean. Let the pudding rest in the steamer, on a wire rack, for 10 minutes before turning it out onto a serving plate.

RUM AND BUTTER SAUCE

1. In a medium saucepan, melt the butter and add the brown sugar. Cook over medium heat for a few minutes, until the brown sugar dissolves with the butter and begins to become foamy.

2. Whisk in the rum. Be careful, this will steam up quickly.

3. When smooth, add the vanilla extract and cream.

4. Simmer slowly for 5-7 minutes until the sauce slightly thickens. You want the temperature to be near soft-ball stage on a candy thermometer or around 220–225°F. Serve warm over the figgy pudding.

Strawberries and Cream Sherry Trifle

PREP TIME: **60** MINUTES + STANDING TIME | COOK TIME: **45** MINUTES | SERVES **16**

SPONGE CAKE

6 large or extra-large **eggs**
(room temperature is best)

1 cup **white sugar**

1 tbsp **vanilla extract**

1 cup **flour**, sifted

2 tbsp **melted salted butter**

VANILLA CUSTARD

3 cups **whole milk**

⅓ cup + 1 tbsp **flour**

⅔ cup **sugar**

pinch of **salt**

3 slightly beaten extra-large
egg yolks

2 tbsp **butter**

2 tsp **vanilla extract**

VANILLA WHIPPED CREAM

1½ cups **whipping cream**

4 rounded tbsp **icing sugar**
(powdered sugar)

1 tsp **vanilla extract**

STRAWBERRIES AND SWEET SHERRY

2 lbs fresh **strawberries**

½ cup **white sugar**

½ cup **sweet sherry**

This sherry trifle is another throwback to my childhood years with a simplified and updated approach. The trifles of my Sunday dinner memories didn't always have a boozy element, but the layers of cake, custard, fruit, jelly, and cream were my idea of absolute heaven. As soon as I began to bake, I started inventing versions of my own, and I'm still doing it to this day. This recipe concentrates on 4 main elements—sponge cake, vanilla custard, fresh strawberries, and whipped cream—and is a wonderful way to serve dessert to a large gathering any time during the Christmas season.

SPONGE CAKE

1. Preheat oven to 325°F.

2. Line the bottom of a 9- or 10-inch springform pan with parchment paper but do NOT grease the sides. Greasing the sides will not allow the cake to rise well, and since the cake is cooled in the pan, the ungreased sides provide support for the cake as it cools so it will not shrink.

3. In the bowl of an electric mixer, using a whisk attachment, combine the eggs, sugar, and vanilla extract and beat on medium-high speed for about 10 minutes until the mixture is foamy and pale in colour.

4. Reduce the speed of the mixer to medium-low and with the mixer running, begin to continuously sprinkle in the rounded tablespoons of flour. Stop the mixer as soon as the flour is fully incorporated.

5. Remove 1 to 2 cups of the sponge-cake batter, and mix it with the melted butter.

6. Immediately add this mixture back into the main batter, folding it in very gently with a rubber spatula. Make sure the

butter mixture is fully mixed in, but be careful not to overmix the batter when folding as this can cause the batter to deflate.

7.   Pour the batter into the prepared 9-inch pan and bake for approximately 45 minutes or until the top springs back fully when pressed lightly. Watch this cake closely as it will overbake easily if left for 5 minutes too long. Start checking it at the 40 minute mark just to be sure, although it always takes the full 45 minutes in my oven.

8.   Cool the cake completely IN THE PAN upside down for at least a couple of hours before carefully and slowly running a sharp knife around the outside edge of the pan to release the cake from the sides. Release the sides of the springform pan and peel the parchment paper off the bottom of the cake. You can then cut the cake in large cubes to use in the trifle.

VANILLA CUSTARD

1.   Scald the milk in the microwave or in a saucepan on the stovetop to almost boiling. Microwave works best as there is no chance of burning the milk.

2.   Meanwhile, in a saucepan, combine the flour, sugar, and salt.

3.   Over medium-low flame, slowly add about ⅓ of the scalded milk, whisking constantly.

4.   As you notice the filling beginning to thicken, add another ⅓ of the scalded milk continuing to stir constantly until it begins to thicken again.

5.   Add the final ⅓ of scalded milk, stirring constantly. Continue to cook over medium-low heat until mixture begins to slightly thicken.

6.   At this point, remove from heat and pour about a half cup of this mixture onto the beaten egg yolks, whisking constantly.

7.   Pour the egg mixture immediately back into the pot, continuing to constantly stir.

8.   Cook for an additional few minutes until the filling reaches pudding consistency and remove from the flame. The mixture should just be beginning to boil at this point.

9.   Stir in the butter and vanilla extract. Cool completely before using in the trifle.

VANILLA WHIPPED CREAM

1.   Whip together the whipping cream, icing sugar, and vanilla extract to firm peaks.

STRAWBERRIES AND SWEET SHERRY

1.   Wash, hull, and slice the strawberries and place them in a glass bowl.

2.   Sprinkle on the ½ cup white sugar and let stand for 60 minutes, tossing the berries several times.

3.   Drain the berry juice from the strawberries but reserve it and mix it with the ½ cup sweet sherry.

to construct the trifle

1. You will need at least a 12-cup trifle bowl or serving bowl to contain this trifle.

2. Take ⅓ of the cake cubes and fit them closely into the bottom of the dish. Sprinkle with ⅓ of the strawberry juice and sherry mixture.

3. Cover with ⅓ of the sliced strawberries followed by ½ of the chilled custard.

4. Add the next layer of cake, strawberry syrup, strawberries, and custard as in steps 2 and 3.

5. Finally, add the last layer of cake cubes and the final sprinkle of strawberry syrup.

6. Top with the Vanilla Whipped Cream and the last of the sliced berries.

7. Chill for several hours or overnight before serving.

Chocolate Raspberry Mille Feuilles

PREP TIME: 60 MINUTES + CHILLING TIME | COOK TIME: 20 MINUTES

MAKES 8 LARGE PASTRIES OR 16 SMALLER SQUARES

This is my kind of dessert for a dinner party at any time during the holiday season. It's utterly delicious, looks fantastic, and is much easier to make than your guests will think. Its elegant appearance belies its simple preparation: from the store-bought puff pastry to easy chocolate filling. It can also be made a day in advance and needs no time or fussy preparation before serving, so you can spend time where you should—at the table with friends and family.

PASTRY

1 lb frozen puff pastry

3 cups fresh raspberries

WHIPPED CHOCOLATE FILLING

2½ cups whipping cream

3 cups dark chocolate chips (50% cacao)

4 rounded tbsp icing sugar (powdered sugar)

1 tsp vanilla extract

CHOCOLATE GANACHE TOP

1 cup chocolate chips (50% cacao)

⅓ cup whipping cream

1 tbsp corn syrup

PASTRY

1. Roll out the puff pastry into three 8-inch squares. Place on parchment-lined cookie sheets. You may have to bake these one at a time depending on the size of your cookie sheet or oven.

2. Dock the pastry by stabbing holes in it with a fork about every ½ inch over the entire surface of the pastry. Place it in the freezer for 10 minutes to ensure it is well chilled. Puff pastry MUST be baked very cold.

3. Preheat oven to 400°F.

4. Place another sheet of parchment paper on top of the pastry and weight it down with another cookie sheet on top. This keeps the pastry from puffing too much and ensures it is crispy when baked.

5. Bake for about 15 minutes. Then decrease the heat to 375°F, remove the top pan and top sheet of parchment paper, and bake for about another 5 minutes or so until it is evenly medium golden brown throughout. Cool the baked pastry sheets completely before filling the layers of the mille feuilles.

WHIPPED CHOCOLATE FILLING

1. To a double boiler, add ¾ cup of the whipping cream and the 3 cups of chocolate chips. Melt them together slowly until smooth. You'll want this mixture to be just at the melting point, so don't overheat it. If it feels too hot to the touch, transfer it to a glass bowl and stir occasionally until it reaches a lukewarm temperature.

2. To the bowl of an electric stand mixer, add the other 1¾ cups whipping cream, icing sugar, and vanilla extract. Whip to firm peaks.

3. Fold the chocolate mixture gently into the whipped cream in about 3 portions. Fold only enough so there are no white streaks in the mixture. The less you fold, the lighter the chocolate filling will be. The chocolate mixture will have to be refrigerated for up to an hour before use. Fold it gently for a couple of turns every 20 minutes.

CHOCOLATE GANACHE TOP

1. Melt together the chocolate chips, whipping cream, and corn syrup until just at the melting point. Pour and spread evenly over the chilled mille feuilles. Chill for another 60 minutes before cutting.

2. Trim all of the edges of the chilled mille feuilles to expose the raspberries at the edges. (The trimmings are the baker's bonus!)

3. Cut the trimmed mille feuilles into 8 individual rectangles or 16 squares. Garnish with additional fresh raspberries and serve.

to construct the mille feuilles

1. Lay the first layer of pastry onto a parchment-lined cookie sheet, cutting board, or in the bottom of a 9x9-inch baking pan with enough parchment paper draping over two opposite sides of the pan to allow you to lift the mille feuilles out of the pan when they are completely chilled.

2. Spread a thin layer of the whipped chocolate over the pastry. Place the raspberries in even rows, ⅛ inch or so apart, over the entire surface of the pastry.

3. Spread enough of the whipped chocolate over the raspberries to completely cover them. You can use a piping bag for this purpose to ensure the raspberries are completely enveloped in chocolate by piping it into the spaces between them.

4. Spread the chocolate just to the tops of the raspberries, removing any excess and making sure the raspberries at the edges are completely covered.

5. Add the next layer of pastry and repeat the process with the raspberries and whipped chocolate before adding the top layer of pastry. Use any excess whipped chocolate to fill any gaps around the edges and to smooth the sides. You don't have to be too fussy about it at this point. The edges will be trimmed later.

6. Chill the mille feuilles for 4 hours or longer before cutting. Overnight is probably best to ensure clean cuts.

Chocolate Orange Cheesecake

PREP TIME: **25** MINUTES | COOK TIME: **60** MINUTES | SERVES **16**

CHOCOLATE ORANGE CHEESECAKE

1½ cups **Oreo cookie crumbs**

⅓ cup **melted butter**

3 tbsp **sugar**

1½ lbs **cream cheese**

1¼ cups **sugar**

3 **eggs**

2 tsp **vanilla extract**

¾ cup **whipping cream**

1½ squares **unsweetened baking chocolate**, melted (In a pinch you can substitute ½ cup cocoa but add another ¼ cup whipping cream to this half of the mixture)

zest of 1 large **orange**, finely grated

GANACHE GLAZE

¼ cup **whipping cream**

1 cup semisweet or dark **chocolate chips**

I know those round chocolate oranges I get in my stocking each year are why I can't help but associate that flavour combination with the holidays. It seems a natural choice to me for the season, so it is one of the reasons this outstanding cheesecake makes it to either my Christmas Day or New Year's Day dinner menu most years. I first started making it about twenty years ago, and it has been a big hit in our family and online at *RockRecipes.com*. Another great thing about desserts like cheesecake during the holidays is they can be made a day or two in advance and will last for several days in the fridge too, so you can share them with as many visitors as you can. They will all want a little slice, believe me!

CHOCOLATE ORANGE CHEESECAKE

1. Preheat oven to 325°F.

2. Lightly grease the bottom but not the sides of a 9- or 10-inch springform pan. Line the bottom with a sheet of parchment paper for easy release from the pan later, once the cheesecake has cooled.

3. Mix together the cookie crumbs, melted butter, and 3 tbsp sugar and press into pan.

4. Cream together the cream cheese and 1¼ cups sugar.

5. Add the eggs, one at a time, mixing well after each addition.

6. Add the vanilla extract and whipping cream and blend until smooth then divide mixture into 2 equal portions in separate bowls.

7. To the first half of the mixture, stir in the melted chocolate (or cocoa and additional cream).

8. Pour into bottom of the prepared springform pan.

9. To the second half of the mixture, stir in the finely grated orange zest. Carefully spoon this mixture over the top of the chocolate mixture already in the pan.

10. Bake for about 60 minutes or until the surface of the cake no longer looks glossy. Remove from oven and immediately run a sharp knife around the edge of the pan to release the cake. Cool completely in the pan. Top with the ganache glaze.

GANACHE GLAZE

1. In a heavy bottomed pot, scald but do not boil the whipping cream then melt in the chocolate chips over low heat.

2. Pour over cooled cake, or to create ganache lace, cool slightly and spoon into a piping bag fitted with a number 3 tip. Pipe over the entire cake in a circular, overlapping swirling pattern, repeating coverage all over the cake until all ganache glaze is used. Garnish with orange segments, orange zest curls, or orange slices.

Strawberry Screech Black Forest Cake

PREP TIME: **30** MINUTES + CHILLING TIME | COOK TIME: **40** MINUTES | SERVES **12-16**

CHOCOLATE CAKE

2 cups **sugar**

2 cups **all-purpose flour**

¾ cup **cocoa**

2 tsp **baking powder**

1 tsp **baking soda**

½ tsp **salt**

2 **eggs**

1 cup **soured milk** (just add a tbsp of lemon juice or vinegar to the milk)

1 cup **cold black coffee**

½ cup **vegetable oil**

2 tsp **vanilla extract**

STRAWBERRY FILLING

4 cups fresh or frozen **strawberries**

¾ cup **sugar**

2 tbsp **cornstarch** dissolved in ¼ cup **cold water**

VANILLA WHIPPED CREAM

4 cups **whipping cream**

6 rounded tbsp **icing sugar** (powdered sugar)

2 tsp **vanilla extract**

CHOCOLATE GANACHE

1 cup **chocolate chips**

¼ cup **whipping cream**

ADDITIONAL

4-6 oz **Newfoundland Screech** (or other good quality dark rum)

I usually make two or more desserts for Christmas Day so I'll have leftovers for entertaining more friends and family on Boxing Day. I cannot count the number of times I've made this particular cake as part of many celebrations over the years, including Christmas. It is one of the most-requested desserts by guests to our home and they are never shy about asking for it during the holidays. This is a cake that's best made a day ahead in order for it to chill properly. Don't worry about the whipped cream, the small amount of cornstarch, in the icing sugar used to sweeten it, acts as an excellent stabilizer, making it last for at least a couple of days.

CHOCOLATE CAKE

1. Preheat oven to 350°F.

2. Combine all ingredients in a mixing bowl and beat with electric mixer for 2 minutes.

3. Pour into 2 greased and floured 9-inch cake pans. Bake for 35-40 minutes or until a toothpick inserted in the center comes out clean.

4. Cool completely. Split cake into 4 layers

5. Bake for about 60 minutes or until the surface of the cake no longer looks glossy. Remove from oven and immediately run a sharp knife around the edge of the pan to release the cake. Cool completely in the pan. Top with the ganache glaze.

STRAWBERRY FILLING

1. Combine the strawberries and sugar in a saucepan and bring to a gentle boil.

2. Thicken with 2 tbsp cornstarch dissolved in ¼ cup cold water, which is added to the strawberries while stirring gently.

3. Boil gently for 1 additional minute, stirring constantly. Divide in 2 portions and cool completely.

VANILLA WHIPPED CREAM

1. Combine all ingredients and whip until stiff mounds form.

CHOCOLATE GANACHE

1. Heat whipping cream to scalding, but do not boil.

2. Stir in chocolate chips and stir over low heat until smooth.

3. You can dip strawberries in this glaze to garnish your cake as well as drizzling it over the cake for the final presentation. I use a piping bag with a number 3 writing tip to drizzle the ganache over the cake, but a Ziploc bag with the corner snipped off works just as well.

❋

to construct the cake

1. Split individual layers of cake into two layers making four layers in total. Sprinkle each layer of cake with about 1 ounce of Screech.

2. Spread a layer of vanilla whipped cream on the first cake layer, followed alternately with a layer of cake, a layer of strawberry filling, cake, then cream again, finishing with the final layer of cake.

3. Frost sides of cake with vanilla whipped cream, and using a piping bag, pipe a border of whipped cream around the top of the cake.

4. Fill the middle of the border on top with the remaining strawberry filling.

5. Decorate the cake as desired with chocolate-ganache-dipped strawberries and a drizzle of chocolate ganache.

Eggnog Bread Pudding *with* Brandy Sauce

5-6 cups **white bread cubes**

1 tsp **freshly grated nutmeg**

1½ cups **whipping cream**

1½ cups **milk**

3 tbsp **brandy** (optional)

3 **eggs**

3 **egg yolks**

⅔ cup **sugar**

1 tbsp **vanilla extract**

pinch **salt**

¼ cup **turbinado sugar** (optional)

For the **Brandy Sauce**
use the same recipe for the
Rum & Butter Sauce on
page 70 but substitute
brandy for the rum.

At some point during the Christmas season, I just have to make one of Spouse's favourites: a soul-warming, decadent, creamy bread pudding. She loves any type of bread pudding, especially if it comes with an indulgent, warm, sweet sauce poured over top. This particular version hits all the right points for a great bread pudding with a festive flair. I like adding a sparkling layer of coarse-grained turbinado sugar on top for a contrasting thin crunchy layer that also adds to its holiday appeal.

1. Remove all the crust from the bread slices and cut them in small cubes or just into half slices. You'll need enough to fill the baking dish you're using, so let that be your guide.

2. Preheat oven to 350°F (325°F for glass bakeware). Grease an 8x8- or 9x9-inch baking dish well.

3. Sprinkle half the nutmeg onto the bread cubes and toss well. Sprinkle on the other half of the nutmeg and toss the cubes again. This helps distribute the nutmeg evenly throughout the pudding.

4. Whisk together the cream, milk, brandy, eggs, egg yolks, sugar, vanilla extract, and salt.

5. Pour the mixture evenly over the bread cubes, pressing down slightly to make sure all the cubes are soaked.

6. Let the pudding stand for 30 minutes to completely absorb the liquid. You can then sprinkle the turbinado sugar on top if you are using it.

7. Bake for about 40-50 minutes until the custard is set and no longer liquid in the center. Let the bread pudding stand for about 20 minutes before serving.

GIFT GIVING

There is really nothing more thoughtful or appreciated than a handmade gift. If that gift comes in the form of a tasty treat to help celebrate Christmas, then you can be assured the appreciation will double. Homemade food gifts may once have been an economical solution for seasonal giving, but with time being the most valuable commodity these days, homemade gifts are truly personal gifts. The recipes that follow are some of the most enjoyed gifts that I've given over the years. They are bound to please many on your Christmas list.

Spiced Clementine & Orange Marmalade

PREP TIME: **30** MINUTES + STANDING TIME | COOK TIME: **2** HOURS **30** MINS

MAKES ABOUT SEVEN **8** OZ JARS

This is another great gift idea to make well in advance of the Christmas season. I've only recently started making homemade marmalade and was surprised how easy it is to prepare. Yes it takes some time because it's done in two stages, but the overall effort is minimal for the outstanding quality of the end product. This version uses seasonal clementines along with the oranges, but you can just substitute more orange if you like. The spices add great flavour and fragrance to this intensely citrus marmalade. Those on your gift list will surely thank you for this thoughtful and tasty present as they spread it on their toast on Christmas morning.

5 large **oranges** (choose oranges neither too thick nor too thin skinned)

6 **clementines**

8 cups **water**

8 cups **sugar**

2 **cinnamon sticks**

¼ tsp **ground cloves**

1 tsp **allspice**

1.   Whether you are using organic citrus fruit or not, wash both the oranges and clementines very well before using them.

2.   Cut each orange and clementine into quarters, then slice the quarters into very thin slices.

3.   In a large pot or Dutch oven, add the slices to the water along with the sugar. (Use only stainless steel or ceramic-lined pots. The acid in the citrus fruit will react with aluminum.)

4.   Slowly bring the mixture to a slow boil, ensuring the sugar is fully dissolved, then remove from the heat and cover the pot.

5.   Leave the mixture in the pot at room temperature overnight.

6.   Next day, add the cinnamon stick, cloves, and allspice to the pot.

7.   Slowly bring the pot to a slow rolling boil for about 2 hours, stirring occasionally.

8.   After 2 hours, increase the heat to about medium and begin to take the temperature of the marmalade. You want to take the mixture to between 220-225°F on a candy thermometer. This is the temperature needed for the pectin to set.

9.   Remove the marmalade from the heat and let it cool before adding it to sterilized mason jars and processing in a water bath to ensure a good seal on the jars as instructed by the bottle manufacturer.

10. Store in a cool dark place.

Decorated Ginger Snaps

PREP TIME: **15** MINUTES + CHILLING TIME | COOK TIME: **13** MINUTES | MAKES **24** COOKIES

Ginger Snaps are our family's favourite cookies to decorate at Christmas, and those decorations need not be complicated to be festive. You can get as creative as you like: colouring the royal frosting, sprinkling on edible glitter, or using silver or gold dragees on top of the royal icing. It's a great pre-Christmas activity to do with the kids too. As you can see from the cookies in the photo, decorated by my daughter, Olivia, a Ziploc bag with the corner cut off is really all you need to add a simple, elegant snowflake pattern. It really couldn't be easier.

GINGER SNAPS

2 cups **flour**

1½ tbsp **ginger**

2 tsp **baking soda**

1 tsp **cinnamon**

½ tsp **salt**

½ cup **shortening**

¼ cup **butter**

½ cup **white sugar**

½ cup **brown sugar**

¼ cup **molasses**

ROYAL ICING

1 large **egg white**

pinch **cream of tartar**

1¼ cups (approx.) **icing sugar** (powdered sugar)

GINGER SNAPS

1. Sift together the flour, ginger, baking soda, cinnamon, and salt and set aside.

2. Cream together the shortening, butter, sugars, and molasses until light and fluffy.

3. Fold in the dry-ingredient mixture until a soft dough forms.

4. Refrigerate for a couple of hours until the dough is well chilled.

5. Preheat oven to 350°F.

6. Roll out to about ⅛ of an inch or a little thicker.

7. Use cookie cutters to cut out the cookies and transfer to a parchment-lined baking sheet.

8. Bake for 15-18 minutes, depending on the size of your cookies. The cookies pictured were made using a 3-inch cookie cutter and took about 17 minutes. You don't want to under bake them or they will not be crispy.

9. Store in airtight containers. Freezes well.

ROYAL ICING

1. Beat together the egg white, cream of tartar and about 1 cup of the icing sugar until light and fluffy.

2. Beat in the remaining icing sugar, a tablespoon at a time, until the icing reaches a spreadable consistency.

3. Use a piping bag, or a Ziploc bag with the corner snipped off, to draw on snowflake patterns or decorate however you like.

Chocolate Toffee Pecan Brittle

PREP TIME: 10 MINUTES + COOLING TIME | **COOK TIME: 10** MINUTES | MAKES ABOUT **3** LBS

2 cups **butter**

2 cups firmly packed **light brown sugar**

2 cups dark chocolate or milk **chocolate chips**

2 cups toasted, roughly chopped **pecans**

With only four ingredients, this incredibly delicious and utterly addictive candy is very quick and simple to prepare. What better homemade Christmas gift could there be?

People are often impressed by getting homemade confections for Christmas, and if they want to think you've fussed over this for hours, let them go right ahead. Some cellophane bags or squares filled with this toffee brittle and tied with a festive ribbon will light up the eyes of the child inside whoever is lucky enough to receive it.

1. This batch makes enough to fill about a cookie sheet, which you should line with parchment paper before you begin. A silicone baking sheet also works very well.

2. Bring the butter and brown sugar to a simmer over medium-low heat or lower. A slow, gentle simmer is what you need or else the candy will harden far too quickly.

3. Watch this very carefully and don't leave it on the stove unattended as it can burn quickly. This mixture also reaches very high temperatures, so be extra careful with it. This is not a recipe to make with kids in the kitchen.

4. When the mixture reaches 300°F on a candy thermometer, immediately pour it onto the parchment- or silicone pad-lined cookie sheet.

5. Using a silicone spatula or wooden spoon, carefully, and working quickly before it hardens, spread the candy mixture evenly over the pan.

6. While still hot, sprinkle on the chocolate chips.

7. Allow the candy to stand for 3 -5 minutes or so to let the chocolate melt then evenly spread it over the surface of the candy.

8. Finally, while the chocolate is still melted, sprinkle on the toasted pecans.

9. Press the nuts down slightly to get good contact with the chocolate.

10. Allow the candy to cool for a couple of hours or overnight before breaking it into pieces. Store in an airtight container.

Bourbon Balls

PREP TIME: **20** MINUTES + CHILLING TIME | COOK TIME: **10** MINUTES | MAKES ABOUT **3** DOZEN

These very simple treats are super easy to put together, and you can make them in a number of variations with your own favourite tipple. Use rum or bourbon, change the hazelnuts to pecans or whatever nuts you like. Add rye whiskey with chopped cherries or other dried fruits, brandy and white chocolate chunks, or coconut with coconut rum. Be creative to make your own signature version or one you know those on your gift list will love. These yummy morsels are perfect for gift giving and should be made at least a day in advance to let the flavours meld.

2¾ cups **vanilla wafer crumbs**

1 cup toasted, roughly chopped **hazelnuts**

1 cup **icing sugar** (powdered sugar)

4 tbsp **cocoa powder**

3 tbsp dark **corn syrup** or **honey**

1 cup **bourbon** (or other favourite spirit)

12–16 oz of **good-quality chocolate**

1. Mix together the cookie crumbs, hazelnuts, icing sugar, cocoa, corn syrup and bourbon well and roll into 1-inch balls. Place the balls on a parchment-lined cookie sheet as you form them and chill in the fridge for at least 60 minutes.

2. When balls are fully chilled, melt the chocolate in a double boiler.

3. Do not let the chocolate overheat. Melt it very gently over slowly simmering water. You want the chocolate just at its melting point before you dip the bourbon balls. Higher temperatures can cause the chocolate to develop white spots when it's fully cooled. Keep the chocolate over the hot water even when you remove it from the stove. I simply use two forks to roll the balls around in the chocolate one at a time; the fork also allows excess chocolate to drip away easily.

4. Drop onto a parchment- or waxed paper-lined cookie sheet and let the chocolate cool at room temperature. Store the balls in an airtight container.

White Chocolate Cranberry Pistachio Biscotti

PREP TIME: **25** MINUTES | COOK TIME: **55** MINUTES | MAKES ABOUT **2** DOZEN

Biscotti is the ideal cookie to make for Christmas gift giving because it can be made two weeks in advance or more. These traditional Italian-inspired treats are twice baked, one in sort of a loosely shaped loaf, then sliced and baked again to crisp them on a cookie sheet. These crisp cookies are meant for dipping in either a cup of good strong coffee or in a glass of sweet wine. The flash of red colour from the cranberries and the bright green of the pistachios both contrast nicely with the white chocolate, making these biscotti particularly festive looking. Wrapped in cellophane and tied with a brightly coloured ribbon, they make an ideal hostess gift, wherever you are invited during the holiday season.

3 cups **flour**

3 tsp **baking powder**

½ tsp **salt**

½ cup **butter**

1 cup **sugar**

3 tsp **vanilla extract**

3 **eggs**

1 cup chopped, **dried cranberries**

1 cup lightly toasted, **unsalted pistachio nuts**

2 cups **white-chocolate chips**

1. Preheat oven to 350°F.

2. Sift together the flour, baking powder, and salt and set aside.

3. Cream together the butter, sugar, and vanilla extract very well until light and fluffy.

4. Beat in the eggs, one at a time, beating well after each addition.

5. Fold in the dry ingredients, just until the flour is incorporated.

6. Work the dough as little as possible for the lightest biscotti. In the final few turns of folding in the flour, just when it's almost completely incorporated, add the cranberries and pistachio nuts.

7. Form the dough into two 3-inch wide logs and place 6 inches apart on a parchment-lined cookie sheet.

8. Bake for about 30 minutes.

9. Remove the biscotti from the oven and let cool for about 10-15 minutes before cutting the biscotti on a diagonal into ¾-inch thick slices.

10. Place the biscotti back on the parchment-lined cookie sheet and reduce the oven temperature to 300°F. Bake for an additional 15 minutes before turning the cookies over and baking for an additional 10 minutes.

11. Cool completely on a wire rack.

12. In a double boiler, melt the white-chocolate chips just to the melting point over slow simmering water.

13. Dip one side of the biscotti into the chocolate and lay them on parchment paper until the chocolate cools and hardens.

Raspberry Chocolate Truffles

PREP TIME: **30** MINUTES + COOLING TIME | MAKES ABOUT **3** DOZEN

You cannot give a gift of chocolate that won't be appreciated. That's basically a universal law. When that chocolate happens to be soft, rich, indulgent truffles you made yourself, you're in for a whole other level of gift gratitude.

I've made all kinds of truffles over the years, flavoured with liqueurs, orange zest, rum, and any number of other spirits. At Christmas, I always gravitate back to making this version with natural raspberry flavour, a perfect pairing with the richness of chocolate. I usually use small, paper candy cups to present them in Christmas tins or holiday themed printed boxes. Don't give them all away though; you'll definitely want to make extras to have on hand for yourself.

2 cups fresh or frozen **raspberries**

¼ cup **icing sugar** (powdered sugar)

1 cup **whipping cream**

20 oz **good-quality chocolate**, chopped (at least 50% cocoa)

2 tbsp **corn syrup**

cocoa for dusting

There are some very good-quality dark-chocolate chips available which can be used in this recipe. 20 ounces of chocolate is equivalent to 3¼ cups of chocolate chips. Just be sure it says a minimum of 50% cocoa on the package.

1. Puree the raspberries and icing sugar together in a food processor or blender. Press the raspberry puree through a fine sieve to remove the seeds. Set the de-seeded puree aside for later.

2. Heat the whipping cream to almost boiling, either in a small saucepan or in the microwave.

3. Chop the chocolate and add it to a double boiler over slowly simmering water. Add the warmed cream and corn syrup, stirring until the chocolate is completely melted and smooth. As soon as it's smooth, take it off the heat. You don't want to overheat the chocolate.

4. Stir in the raspberry puree and transfer the truffle mixture to a glass bowl. Let it cool to almost room temperature before covering it with plastic wrap and cooling completely in the refrigerator for at least a couple of hours or until it is firm.

5. Working quickly, form the truffle mixture into 1-inch balls. I use the smallest of my cookie-dough scoops for this purpose, which is an ideal tool for the job. A melon baller can also serve this purpose.

6. Roll the formed truffles in cocoa and place on a parchment-lined cookie sheet. Chill for 60 minutes before transferring the truffles to airtight containers. These are best stored in the fridge and taken out 20-30 minutes before serving.

TURKEY AND ALL THE TRIMMINGS

Christmas dinner is the highpoint of the annual cooking calendar, but it doesn't need to be the most stressful one. A well-planned meal and good timing are what's most essential to a successful Christmas dinner. Sure, the turkey will always take center stage, but it's the tasty side dishes that people seem to remember most, especially if it's something a little different from what they traditionally know. These recipes will help you plan a celebration Christmas dinner that can keep with tradition while giving the opportunity to create new favourite dishes for Christmases yet to come.

CRANBERRY HAZELNUT TURKEY WELLINGTON

TURKEY
AND TRIMMINGS

Tourtière

PREP TIME: **60** MINUTES + CHILLING TIME | COOK TIME: **60** MINUTES | SERVES **8**

2½ lbs **ground pork shoulder** (coarse grind if possible)

salt and **pepper** to season

2 **celery stalks**, finely diced

1 medium **onion**, finely diced

4 cloves **garlic**, minced

1 cup finely chopped **cremini mushrooms**

1 large **bay leaf**

1 tsp **savoury**

1 tsp chopped **fresh thyme** (or ½ tsp dried thyme)

½ tsp **nutmeg**

½ tsp **cinnamon**

pinch of **ground cloves**

½ tsp **black pepper**

½ tsp **salt**

1½ cups **pork** or **chicken stock**

1 cup grated **raw potato**

1 **egg**

1 tbsp **milk**

For the pastry, I use the same recipe as for **Butter Tarts** found on page 69. You will want to make 1½ times the pastry recipe if you plan on making leaves or other decorations for the top.

Tourtière is very much a French-Canadian tradition at Christmas, served almost universally in Quebec on Christmas Eve. The tradition also exists for many people of Acadian descent in Atlantic Canada and in the Port au Port region on the west coast of Newfoundland where many people are of French ancestry.

It was never a tradition in our family, but after trying several different variations over the years, I've come to look forward to making this hearty meat pie just before Christmas. It's never too late to start a new Christmas tradition.

1. I like to make my filling the day before and chill it in the fridge overnight before adding it to the pie crust. I also grind my own pork shoulder for this recipe using a meat grinder attachment on my electric mixer. If you can't grind your own, ask your butcher if they can coarse grind some pork shoulder for you. The coarse grind makes for a much meatier textured tourtière.

2. In a large, heavy-bottomed Dutch oven, season the ground pork with salt and pepper and brown it quickly over high heat. Drain off the excess fat and remove the meat from the pan.

3. Add the celery, onion, garlic, and chopped mushrooms to the pot and cook until the onions are softened but not browned.

4. Add the browned pork back to the Dutch oven along with the bay leaf, savoury, thyme, nutmeg, cinnamon, cloves, pepper, salt, and stock. Simmer very slowly, stirring occasionally, until practically all the liquid has disappeared from the pan. Remove from the heat, stir in the grated potato, and cool completely.

5. On a well-floured surface, roll out ½ of the pastry to about a 12-inch circle and fit into the bottom of a 9- to 10-inch pie plate.

6. Roll out the top crust to about 2 inches larger than the top of your pie plate. Add the cooled filling and add the top crust, cutting a small circle out of the pastry's center to allow steam to escape.

7. Tuck the top crust under the bottom crust at the edges of the pie plate and crimp or flute the edges of the crust to seal. Brush with an egg wash made by whisking together 1 egg and 1 tbsp milk. (You will not use all this egg wash.)

8. Decorate as desired by cutting shapes like leaves out of extra pastry if desired. I score the tops of the leaf shapes with the tip of a sharp knife to create the veining in the leaves. Small Christmas cookie cutters also make good pastry decorations for a tourtière. Chill the pie for 30 minutes before putting it into the oven. You can also prepare the entire pie a day in advance and bake it on the day you are serving it.

9. Preheat the oven to 375°F and bake for 20 minutes, then reduce the heat to 250°F and bake for an additional 30-40 minutes until the crust is an even golden brown. If the edges brown too quickly, cover them with thin strips of aluminum foil.

10. Let the tourtière rest for 20 minutes before serving.

Orange and Clove Brined Roast Turkey

PREP TIME: **30** MINUTES + BRINING TIME | COOK TIME: **2** HOURS **30** MINUTES | SERVES **10–12** WITH LEFTOVERS

ORANGE CLOVE BRINED ROAST TURKEY
You'll need a food-grade plastic bucket or large pan, big enough to completely submerge the turkey in the brine, for this recipe.

10–12 lb **fresh turkey**

2 tbsp of **butter**

1 **onion**, quartered

2 **cloves garlic**, sliced

1 whole **orange**, punctured with a fork several times

melted butter for basting

BRINE MIXTURE
6 quarts of **water** (enough to cover the turkey completely)

⅓ cup **table salt**

½ cup **sugar**

¼ cup **honey**

8 whole **cloves**

1 large **onion**, sliced

3 **cloves garlic**, sliced thin

zest and **juice of 2 large oranges**

3 tbsp **whole black peppercorns**

If you've never tried brining a turkey before roasting it, you may be in for a surprise at just how much better it can be. The brining process infuses moisture, seasoning, and subtle flavour to the flesh for the juiciest, most succulent turkey ever. The subtle hints of cloves and orange in this recipe make if perfect for Christmas.

1. In a bucket, combine the water, table salt, sugar, and honey, stirring well to completely dissolve the sugar and salt. Then add the cloves, onion, garlic, orange juice and zest, and black peppercorns.

2. Wash the turkey well and completely submerge it in the bucket of brine. A plate with a couple of heavy cans of tomatoes or beans placed over the turkey will help keep it submerged. Place in the refrigerator overnight or for at least 6-8 hours. I remove one of the shelves in the fridge to make space for the bucket.

3. After brining the turkey, remove it from the brine and pat it dry with paper towels. Preheat the oven to 400°F. Place the turkey on a rack in a roasting pan and truss the turkey with butcher twine (or just tuck the wing tips under the turkey and tie the legs together to simplify things). There's no need to add additional salt or pepper, the brine has already seasoned the meat throughout. Rub the surface of the turkey with a couple of tablespoons of butter. To the cavity add the quartered onion, sliced garlic, and the whole orange.

4. Do not cover the turkey. Open roast the turkey in the preheated oven for 30 minutes before reducing the temperature to 350°F. Brush the turkey with melted butter about every 30-45 minutes to get a nicely browned skin. After reducing the heat, continue roasting for about an additional 2 hours or until the internal temperature of the

Cranberry Hazelnut Turkey Wellington

PREP TIME: **25** MINUTES | COOK TIME: **60** MINUTES | SERVES **16**

2 **cloves garlic**, minced

¼ cup chopped **onion**

1 tbsp **olive oil**

2 tbsp **butter**

2 cups **dry bread crumbs**

½ cup chopped **hazelnuts**

1½ tbsp dry chopped **fresh thyme**

½ cup fresh or frozen **cranberries**

salt and **pepper** to season

3 tbsp (approx.) **turkey** or **chicken stock**

2 sheets, (12x12 inches) **frozen puff pastry**, thawed

1½–2 lbs **uncooked turkey breast**

1 **egg** + 2 tbsp **water** (beaten together for an egg wash)

Here's a terrific festive entertaining idea for any day during the holidays. I've heard from several *Rock Recipes* followers over the years who don't want or need to have all those turkey leftovers and are looking for an alternative to a traditional stuffed turkey. This is an ideal solution, especially for couples, small families, or for dinner party entertaining. It's like Christmas baked into a beautiful puff pastry crust, which makes a stunningly gorgeous presentation when you bring it to the table to carve.

1. Begin by sautéing the garlic and onions in the olive oil and butter for a minute or two.

2. Add the bread crumbs and toss until they begin to brown slightly. Add the hazelnuts, thyme, cranberries, salt, and pepper. Add only enough turkey stock to make the stuffing hold together.

3. Place the first pastry sheet on a parchment-lined cookie sheet. Place the turkey breast along the center line of the pastry sheet. Brush the edges of the pastry with the egg wash.

4. Place the stuffing on top of the turkey. Place the second pastry sheet over the turkey and stuffing. Trim the edges to form an oval shape. Save the trimmings in the fridge.

5. Bring the edges of the dough together by pinching them together to seal. Roll the dough from the bottom layer over the top layer and press down all the way around the perimeter of the pastry. This creates a tighter seal.

6. Brush the egg wash over the entire surface of the pastry. Decorate with additional pastry leaf shapes if desired. Just cut leaf shapes out of the trimmed pastry and score leaf veining into them with the tip of a sharp knife. Cut four ½-inch slots in the top of the pastry to let steam escape. Chill for 20 minutes or longer in the fridge before baking. This helps the pastry to puff.

7. Preheat oven to 400°F for about 15-20 minutes then reduce the heat to 350°F and continue baking for about another 35-45 minutes. Use a meat thermometer to make sure the center has reached at least 170°F to be sure the turkey is completely cooked. Let rest for 10 minutes before cutting into individual servings.

Newfoundland Dressing
(Savoury Stuffing)

While I'm well known in our family circles for pushing the traditional boundaries of a Newfoundland Christmas dinner, there's one thing I don't really experiment with on the occasion—the dressing for the turkey. This simple savoury, onion, and breadcrumb stuffing is a decades old tradition in Newfoundland, and you'd be hard pressed to find many homes where it isn't present at Christmas dinner.

Family recipes vary slightly, some preferring a drier stuffing, some liking it more buttery or a little moister so it holds together better. It can be used to stuff the turkey cavity, of course, but I find that a turkey will cook faster and juicier without being stuffed, so these days we most often use the casserole method to slow cook it in the oven. Once the delicious turkey gravy gets poured on, nobody will know the difference.

½ small **onion**, chopped

2 **clove garlic**, minced (optional)

½ cup **butter**

8 cups **coarse breadcrumbs**

4 or more tbsp **dried savoury**

salt and **pepper** to season

¾-1 cup **chicken stock** (or turkey stock)

1. In a small skillet, slowly sauté the chopped onion (and garlic if desired) in the butter over low heat until the onions are soft but not browned.

2. Meanwhile combine the breadcrumbs, savoury, salt, and pepper in a large bowl. Add the cooked onions and chicken stock and toss well to combine all the ingredients.

3. Use as a stuffing for your Christmas turkey or for any poultry, including game birds.

4. To cook the dressing in the oven, just place it in a covered casserole dish, preheat your oven to 250-300°F for about 30 minutes. Toss the stuffing several times during the cooking time. You may want to add a little more stock when using this method.

Roasted Potatoes

PREP TIME: **15** MINUTES | COOK TIME: **90** MINUTES | SERVES **4–6**

My love of roasted potatoes started many years ago when I began watching more and more Christmas cooking shows out of the UK. While plain boiled potatoes is what you'll most likely find at Christmas dinner in Newfoundland, the British tradition is to make "roasties" and it is one our family has whole-heartedly adopted. The plain boiled potato cannot hold a candle to the crispy-jacketed roast potato with a steaming, fluffy inside. It is a thing of pure, simple perfection.

They are now our family's potatoes of choice with any roast supper and an absolute must-have for Christmas dinner.

---

6 medium-sized **russet potatoes**, peeled

¼ cup **olive oil** (a butter/olive oil combination is very good too)

½ tsp **kosher salt**

½ tsp **cracked black pepper**

1 **whole garlic bulb** broken into about 4 pieces (optional)

1. Parboil the potatoes in salted water for about 5 minutes. Some people prefer to boil them longer; up to 8 minutes or so. This will produce a thicker and crispier jacket to the potato if you prefer.

2. Preheat your oven to 375°F and then heat a baking pan of sufficient size to hold your potatoes without crowding them. A glass or metal pan is fine as long as it is well-heated beforehand. This will help to prevent the potatoes from sticking to the pan.

3. After parboiling, drain the potatoes and let them stand for 5 minutes to steam off. Then toss the potatoes with the olive oil, salt, pepper, and garlic cloves.

4. Transfer the seasoned potatoes, garlic, and oil to the hot baking pan. These should sizzle as they hit the pan: a good indication they will not stick.

5. Roast the potatoes for about 75-90 minutes or until they are nicely golden brown all over. After the first 10 minutes, give the pan a shake to make sure the potatoes are not stuck to it and then turn them every 20 minutes or so.

6. The roasted garlic will have to be removed before the potatoes are finished as it generally cooks faster. 45 minutes or less should be enough to fully cook the roasted garlic.

Maple Roasted Vegetables

PREP TIME: **20** MINUTES | COOK TIME: **60** MINUTES | SERVES **4–6**

Your Christmas dinner table should feature nothing but the best, and that includes all the delicious side dishes too. This recipe is often the main vegetable side dish for our turkey dinners at any time of the year, but is especially welcome and festive at Christmas. It is worth a visit to your neighbourhood farmers market to purchase the best local vegetables you can find for this simple recipe. The freshest and best your local farms have to offer really does make a difference here.

2 carrots, thickly sliced

2 parsnips, thickly sliced

1 large red onion, cut in wedges

1 lemon

1 small butternut squash, cut in chunks

4 cloves garlic, unpeeled

6 yellow beets, quartered

4 tbsp olive oil

pinch salt

pinch black pepper

2–3 tbsp pure maple syrup

1. Toss all of the ingredients, except the maple syrup, together with the olive oil.

2. Preheat oven to 350°F.

3. Roast in a single layer for approximately 30 minutes.

4. Remove from the oven and squeeze the roasted lemon over the rest of the vegetables (careful, it's hot) and then add the maple syrup.

5. Toss together well to coat all the vegetables and roast for about another 30 minutes or until all of the vegetables are fork tender.

6. Toss the vegetables several times during the last of the cooking time to glaze the vegetables in the maple syrup.

Brussels Sprouts
with Prosciutto and Raisins

PREP TIME: **10** MINUTES | COOK TIME: **15** MINUTES | SERVES **6–8**

Brussels sprouts are a traditional side dish for many at Christmas dinner, but it's not always easy to get folks to like them, especially kids. My solution is often to dress up the less popular vegetables with sweet and salty elements that compliment their flavour. The cured prosciutto ham and sweet raisins fill those roles beautifully in this dish. I sometimes use crumpled crisp bacon and toasted nuts in such vegetable medleys too, so experiment with your favourite dried fruits and nuts to create your own signature version of this delicious side dish.

2 lbs **fresh Brussels sprouts**, ends trimmed and cut in half

¼ cup **salted butter**

4 cloves **garlic**, minced

1 cup **golden raisins**

3 oz thinly sliced **prosciutto**, cut in slivers

juice of ½ **lemon**

1 tsp **cracked black pepper**

1. Boil the sprouts in salted water for 5 minutes or until just fork tender before dropping them directly into a bowl of ice water to stop the cooking action.

2. In a large sauté pan, add a couple of tablespoons of the butter and the garlic. Cook for only a minute or two to soften the garlic, but do not brown it.

3. Add the raisins and prosciutto and sauté for just a minute or so before adding the cooked Brussels sprouts and the remaining butter.

4. Toss together over high heat for only a few minutes until the sprouts are warmed through.

5. Turn off the heat, toss in the lemon juice and pepper and serve immediately.

Citrus Fig Cranberry Sauce

PREP TIME: **10** MINUTES | COOK TIME: **30** MINUTES | MAKES ABOUT **3** CUPS

What's turkey without cranberry sauce? It would be like not serving gravy with the meal. There's no need to serve it out of a can though because homemade cranberry sauce is one of the easiest things to prepare with your roast turkey dinner. This recipe adds some sweet figs and balancing citrus and spice flavours to the sauce for the holidays. These traditional festive Christmas flavours give very complimentary yet not overwhelming notes to the sauce.

If you make a large batch before Christmas and bottle it properly in mason jars, this recipe makes another terrific gift-giving idea.

3 cups fresh or frozen cranberries

1 cup chopped dried figs

juice of 1 orange

juice of 1 lemon

½ tsp finely minced orange zest

½ tsp finely minced lemon zest

1 cup water

¼ cup brown sugar

½ cup white sugar

¼ tsp cinnamon

1 star anise (optional)

1. Simmer all of the ingredients together slowly for 30-40 minutes or until the cranberries are fully cooked and the mixture reduces and thickens to a jam-like consistency.

2. Stir the sauce often as it simmers.

3. Remove the star anise, if you used one, and store in mason jars or in plastic containers in the fridge until served.

Caramelized Onion Gravy

PREP TIME: **15** MINUTES | COOK TIME: **40** MINUTES | MAKES ABOUT **8** CUPS

3 qts homemade (or low-sodium) **chicken** or **turkey stock**

2 tbsp **extra virgin olive oil**

2 tbsp **butter**

1½ lbs chopped **Spanish onion**

2 large **shallots**, chopped

4 **cloves garlic**, minced

1 tsp **ground thyme** or **sage** (or 2 tsp chopped fresh thyme or sage)

1 tsp **fresh ground nutmeg**

salt and **pepper** to season

Substitute rosemary for the thyme and use beef stock to make an outstanding beef and onion gravy to serve with prime rib for New Year's dinner.

Getting the gravy right is an essential part of a great Christmas dinner. Everyone always remembers great gravy. This is a very adaptable recipe that I've even made as a vegetarian gravy using vegetable stock and no pan drippings from the turkey. If you are serving both vegetarians and meat eaters at your table, a good idea is to make the gravy in advance and split it into 2 portions: one to serve as-is and one that you can add to the pan drippings to make a turkey and onion gravy. Either way, the deep intense flavour of this complimentary gravy is what your guests will remember.

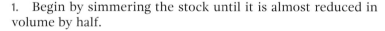

1. Begin by simmering the stock until it is almost reduced in volume by half.

2. Heat the olive oil and butter over medium heat in a sauté pan and add the onions, shallots, and garlic. Cook until the onions soften, caramelize, and turn golden brown, tossing constantly every 2 or 3 minutes. I reduce the heat several times during this process. This can take considerable time: 30 minutes or longer. The more you caramelize the onions, the better the flavour of your gravy.

3. Add the caramelized onion to the reduced stock along with the thyme (or sage) and nutmeg. Simmer for only a few minutes before thickening the gravy by whisking in a slurry made from a couple of tablespoons of flour dissolved into ¾ cup water.

4. At this point, you can serve the gravy with whole pieces of onion, or if you prefer, you can blend it to a smoother consistency using an immersion blender or in small batches in a food processor. Makes about 2 quarts and freezes well in small airtight plastic containers.

Garlic and Lemon Duchess Potatoes

PREP TIME: **45** MINUTES | COOK TIME: **30** MINUTES | SERVES **6-8**

This makes a terrific side dish for Christmas dinner because it's a great way to serve a flavourful version of mashed potatoes that can be prepared a little in advance and one that helps you manage oven space. Once you get the prepared potatoes into the baking dish, they can sit aside for a couple of hours and then be popped into a hot oven while the turkey rests before carving. You'll find this side dish a big help for roast dinners all year round.

4 cloves **roasted garlic**

pinch of **salt**

drizzle **olive oil** (for lemon and garlic roasting)

½ **roasted lemon**, juiced

3 lbs **red or yellow potatoes**

4 tbsp **melted butter**

¼ tsp **black pepper**

½ tsp **salt**

4 **egg yolks**

⅓ cup **cold whipping cream**

1. Preheat oven to 350°F.

2. Place garlic cloves in a garlic roaster or just wrap in aluminum foil with a pinch of salt and a light drizzle of olive oil.

3. In a small glass baking dish, drizzle a little olive oil then place the lemon, cut side down. Roast with the garlic for 45 minutes or so or until the garlic has softened.

4. Meanwhile, peel and cut your potatoes into chunks and simmer gently until fully cooked and fork tender. Drain.

5. Mash the potatoes well and add the butter, juice from the roasted lemon, roasted garlic, salt, and pepper. Mash until smooth.

6. Preheat oven to 375°F.

7. Whisk together the egg yolks and whipping cream. Quickly mix into the mashed potatoes. Turn into a greased baking dish and bake for about 30 minutes or until the top turns golden brown.

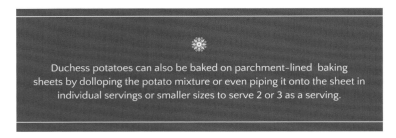

❄

Duchess potatoes can also be baked on parchment-lined baking sheets by dolloping the potato mixture or even piping it onto the sheet in individual servings or smaller sizes to serve 2 or 3 as a serving.

Partridgeberry Molasses Duff

PREP TIME: **20** MINUTES | COOK TIME: **2** HOURS | SERVES **8**

A duff is most often a steamed pudding, cooked either in a cloth bag or in a steamer, and is another must-have for Christmas in my extended family. Some families, mine included, serve duff as a side dish, right on your Christmas dinner plate beside the turkey. While this sweet addition to the plate seems odd to many, I grew up particularly loving my grandmother's steamed raisin duff, which was boiled in a cotton bag in the pot with the vegetables. We still make it today.

Other varieties of duff, like this partridgeberry and molasses version, are more often served as a dessert with a sweet sauce in many parts of Newfoundland. Cranberries or dried fruit like raisins or currents are easily substituted for the partridgeberries (lingonberries). The rum and butter sauce from our Figgy Pudding recipe on page 70 would go well with this dessert, as would a simple butterscotch sauce which is basically the same sauce, minus the rum.

½ cup **molasses**

½ cup **butter**

1 **egg**

1 tsp **pure vanilla extract**

1½ cups **flour**

1½ tsp **baking powder**

½ tsp **baking soda**

1 tsp **cinnamon** (optional)

½ cup **milk**

1½ cups **frozen partridgeberries**

1.   Prepare your steamer by greasing it well and lightly dusting with flour. You will need a 7 cup or larger steamer for this pudding. I sometimes use a heat-proof Pyrex bowl covered tightly in plastic wrap with an outside layer of aluminum foil. I've also used a Bundt pan many times as a steamer. The only caution is to make sure the hole in the center is completely plugged or the pudding will get wet. A wine cork of the right size, or some balled-up plastic wrap stuffed in the hole, will work well for this purpose. Again, the top should be covered tightly with plastic wrap and then a layer of aluminum foil before placing it into the boiling water. The pot that you place your steamer in should be about 1½ times the size of the steamer and should have a metal trivet on the bottom. Do not let your pudding steamer touch the bottom of the pot. An old stoneware tea plate can make an adequate trivet if necessary. Bring about 2 inches of water to a slow simmer in the pot to get it ready.

2.   Cream the molasses and butter well then beat in the egg and vanilla extract. In a separate small bowl, sift together the flour, baking powder, baking soda and cinnamon (if you are using it).

3.   Fold the dry ingredients alternately with the milk into the creamed mixture, beginning and ending with the dry

ingredients. As a general rule, I add the dry ingredients in 3 equal portions and the milk in 2 equal portions.

4. When the last of the dry ingredients is almost incorporated, fold in the partridgeberries as well.

5. Spread the batter evenly into the prepared steamer. Add the cover to the steamer (or a layer each of plastic wrap, then aluminum foil to stop water seeping in).

6. Place the steamer on the trivet at the bottom of the boiling water and place the lid on the pot. Steam the pudding for 2 hours. Test it to see if a wooden toothpick inserted in the center comes out clean.

7. Let the pudding rest in the steamer, on a wire rack, for 10 minutes before turning it out onto a serving plate.

TURKEY LEFTOVERS

Deep Fried Turkey

PREP TIME: **10** MINUTES | COOK TIME: **10** MINUTES | SERVES UP TO **6**

This is a very nostalgic recipe for me, not so much as a Christmas recipe but as a fond remembrance of a special treat from my childhood. Long before frying a whole bird in gallons of oil in your backyard became trendy or fashionable, deep fried turkey meant batter-fried turkey to many of us. I first had a version of this recipe decades ago at Marshall's Restaurant on Water Street in Bay Robert's. Marshall's Restaurant is long gone, but this recipe idea survives as a standard post-holiday or anytime leftover turkey meal in my family. Some in your family might even prefer these leftovers to the traditional roast turkey! We love to serve it with french fries, leftover gravy, dressing, and cranberry sauce.

1 cup **all-purpose flour**

1 cup **rice flour**

½ tsp **salt**

¼ tsp **white pepper**

1 large **egg**, lightly beaten

2¼ cups **cold beer or soda water** (club soda)

3–4 lbs of thick-cut sliced **leftover turkey**

canola oil for deep frying

1. Combine dry ingredients. Add the egg and soda water or beer and whisk together just until the liquid is incorporated. Small lumps in the batter are not a problem.

2. Slice leftover roast turkey into thick slices.

3. Preheat the canola oil in your deep fryer to 375°F.

4. Dip the turkey pieces into plain flour and then into the batter and carefully drop them into the deep fryer.

5. Fry for a few minutes, just until golden brown on both sides.

6. Drain on a wire rack placed over a cookie sheet. Serve immediately.

7. If you have to fry the turkey in more than one batch at a time, hold the fried pieces in a 200°F oven on the draining rack to provide air circulation all the way around the fried turkey pieces to prevent it from getting soggy.

Turkey Parmesan Baked Rotini

PREP TIME: **30** MINUTES | COOK TIME: **45-60** MINUTES | SERVES **8**

WHITE SAUCE

12½ cups **whole milk**

1½ cups **turkey stock**

⅓ cup **butter**

3 tbsp **flour**

¼ tsp **black pepper**

½ tsp **sea salt**

2 tbsp **dry summer savoury**
(or 1 tsp dry thyme)

2 tbsp **Dijon mustard**

TURKEY PARMESAN BAKED ROTINI

3 cups **uncooked rotini pasta**

3 cups **leftover cooked turkey,**
cut in chunks

1 cup **freshly grated parmesan
cheese**

1 cup chopped **button mushrooms**
(optional)

1 large **roasted red pepper,**
chopped (optional)

8 slices **precooked bacon,**
cut in small pieces

3 cups grated **low-fat mozzarella
cheese**

This is probably the most popular leftover turkey recipe to ever appear on *RockRecipes.com*. People just love the rich, creamy pasta with bacon and chunks of turkey, all baked with a cheesy top layer. It's the sort of comfort food that makes winter suppers eagerly anticipated by all.

We always make turkey stock from the carcass of the roast turkey, so this leftover meal, using the last of the leftover turkey along with the freshly made turkey stock, is usually made on that stock-making day. This recipe is one you'll want to keep close at hand because it works equally well with the leftovers from a roast chicken dinner at any time of year.

WHITE SAUCE

1. In the microwave oven, scald the milk and turkey stock until almost boiling.

2. In a medium saucepan over medium heat, cook together the butter, flour, pepper, and salt for 2 minutes.

3. Whisking constantly, slowly pour in the scalded milk and turkey stock. Continue to cook for 2 more minutes stirring constantly.

4. Stir in the savoury and mustard. Set the sauce aside.

TURKEY PARMESAN BAKED ROTINI

1. Cook the pasta just to al dente in boiling salted water. Drain and set aside.

2. Preheat oven to 350°F.

3. Grease the bottom and sides of a large casserole dish.

4. Place half of the cooked rotini pasta in the bottom of the dish.

5. Layer the casserole with half the turkey, half the parmesan cheese, half the mushrooms, half the red pepper, half the bacon, and half the sauce.

6. Repeat these layers and top with the grated mozzarella cheese.

7. Bake for about 45-60 minutes or until the casserole is bubbling and the top is golden brown.

Turkey Sage and Roasted Vegetable Soup

PREP TIME: **20** MINUTES | COOK TIME: **60** MINUTES | SERVES **8**

Leftover turkey is never a problem in our house, especially for Spouse who's a big fan of leftover turkey soup. I always say we're "a turkey ahead" at our place because we make homemade turkey stock from the leftover turkey carcass and neck every time we roast a turkey. We most often use it in a delicious soup, but some gets frozen in small plastic airtight containers to use in soups and other recipes, and some of it always gets used to help make the gravy on the occasion of our next roast turkey dinner. That's my "great gravy" secret.

This soup is a fantastic recipe for the day you make your turkey stock. Turkey stock normally simmers slowly for a couple of hours, which leaves plenty of time to peel, chop, and roast the vegetables before a quick simmer to complete the soup.

4 large **carrots**, peeled and sliced

3 large **parsnip**, peeled and sliced

1 cup diced **turnip**

1 large **onion**, diced

2 stalks **celery**, sliced

3 large **tomatoes**, diced large

4 **cloves garlic**, roughly chopped

3 tbsp **olive oil**

salt and **pepper** to season

8 cups **turkey stock**

2 tbsp finely chopped **fresh sage**

3 cups **leftover roast turkey**, diced or shredded

2 cups **baby spinach leaves**

1. Preheat the oven to 375°F.

2. Toss all the vegetables, tomatoes, and garlic together with the olive oil and season with salt and pepper.

3. Roast in a shallow pan or on a baking sheet in a single layer for about 45 minutes or until the edges of the vegetables just begin to turn brown and caramelize.

4. Transfer the vegetables to a soup pot and add the turkey stock and sage.

5. Season again with salt and pepper if necessary and simmer for only about 20 minutes.

6. In the last 5 minutes of cooking time, add the leftover turkey.

7. Remove the soup from the heat, and just before serving, stir the spinach leaves into the pot. Alternatively, you can add some spinach leaves to each of the bowls before ladling in the soup. This is an especially good idea if you expect to have leftover soup for serving later. It is always best to add the spinach at the last minute before serving to preserve the colour, which makes for a much nicer presentation.

Turkey Cottage Pie

At our house, we make this incredibly tasty turkey cottage pie completely from the leftovers of a turkey dinner. You can make it in one large casserole dish or even in large individual gratin dishes: whatever works. I don't even include measurements for this recipe because they're quite unimportant. Just use what you can fit into whatever baking dish you're using.

And if you're missing an ingredient, don't worry! Just improvise. Make a new small batch of mashed potatoes if you're out of leftovers or use the tasty sliced potato method instead. I actually like that one better. No leftover vegetables? Use frozen veggies in a pinch. No stuffing? Just forget about it and use the other leftovers. It will still be delicious no matter what.

---

leftover turkey, cut in chunks

leftover gravy

leftover stuffing

leftover vegetables (leftover roasted veggies are particularly good.)

leftover mashed potato, warmed with a little milk added (or sliced potatoes as described in the instructions)

a few tbsp melted butter

1. Cover the bottom of the dish with chunks of turkey in a double layer. Pour the gravy over the turkey to cover it. Don't add too much gravy to this pie or, if you are using mashed potatoes, the layers may not stay distinct. It's better to serve extra gravy on the side if you have a lot of it.

2. Next, add a layer of roasted carrots and parsnip or other leftover vegetables.

3. If you have leftover stuffing, add that next. It provides a very good insulating layer between the gravy and potatoes, helping to keep the layers distinct. But if you don't have any, it's not a deal breaker for this versatile recipe.

4. Finally, you can spread on the mashed-potato layer. Run a fork lightly over the surface to create lines or a grid pattern to hold the melted butter, helping it brown better. If you want to be "fancy," transfer your mashed potato to a Ziploc bag and snip the corner off with a pair of sharp scissors and use the bag to pipe the mashed potato in little peaks or swirls all over the surface of the pie.

5. Preheat your oven to 350°F, and drizzle the top of the mashed potatoes with a few tablespoons of melted butter. Pop the pie into the oven and bake until the top is golden and the gravy starts to bubble.

6. For the sliced potato top instead, use about 1 large potato per person. Peel and cut the potatoes into ¼-inch slices. Parboil the sliced potatoes in lightly salted water for about 4 minutes.

7. Drain the potatoes and cool the slices on a cookie sheet until they are able to be handled.

8. Overlap the potatoes all over the surface of the cottage pie and brush them with melted butter before popping the baking dish into a pre-heated 350°F oven until the top begins to brown, the potatoes are fork tender, and the gravy beneath is bubbling, about 40-50 minutes depending on the size of your casserole dish. Smaller individual serving dishes will only need 20-30 minutes, again depending on the size.

Leftover Turkey Chili

PREP TIME: **20** MINUTES | COOK TIME: **30–35** MINUTES | SERVES **4**

4 cloves **garlic**, minced

1 large **red onion**, diced

3 tbsp **olive oil**

1 cup **beer**

28 oz can **crushed tomatoes**

14 oz can **tomato sauce**

2 large **tomatoes**, diced

1 large **roasted red pepper**, peeled and diced small

½–1 whole **jalapeño pepper**, finely minced (optional)

1 tsp **kosher salt**

1 tsp **coarse-ground black pepper**

5 tbsp **chili powder** (more or less to taste)

3 tbsp **smoked paprika**

3 tbsp **ground cumin**

6 tbsp **molasses**

1 can **kidney beans** (or 1½ cups of your favourite cooked beans)

1 cup **frozen corn**

3–4 cups **leftover diced turkey**

One of the most successful ways to deal with any kind of leftover meat is to incorporate it into an already favourite meal. That's exactly what we do with leftover turkey on many occasions, and there's no better example than this comfort food chili with big chunks of turkey. It's a hearty meal with little effort. The only caution when adding cooked poultry to chili, or even spaghetti sauce as we sometimes do, is not to add it until the last of the cooking time. The turkey is already cooked after all, so it really needs only 5 or 10 minutes simmering in the rich tomato sauce to warm it through: any longer and you risk the meat chunks being too dry. This is another recipe to use year round with leftover chicken too.

1.   In a large pot, sauté together onions and garlic in the olive oil for a few minutes. When the onions are softened, add all of the additional ingredients **except** the diced turkey.

2.   Simmer the chili slowly for about 30 minutes, stirring occasionally, before adding the leftover turkey. Simmer again for only a few minutes to heat the turkey. Serve atop steamed rice or in bowls with some of the delicious Bacon Cheddar Cornbread Muffins from page 154 on the side.

Turkey Bubble and Squeak

PREP TIME: **10** MINUTES | COOK TIME: **20–30** MINUTES

SERVES AS MANY AS YOUR LEFTOVERS ALLOW

People from the UK are always surprised to find that we use the term "Bubble and Squeak" here in Newfoundland. Many Newfoundlanders grew up eating Bubble and Squeak as a Monday staple meal using the leftovers from Sunday dinner. Often fried in rendered fat-back pork, the leftovers made a one-pan hash that incorporated any leftover potatoes, vegetables, salt meat, or anything else that could be thrown in.

A post-Christmas Bubble and Squeak can be a great treat for Boxing Day, especially if there's leftover turkey gravy to pour on. If you're hosting a Boxing Day brunch, serve this delicious hash with a poached or over-easy egg on top. Delicious!

---

1 **onion**, diced fine

3–4 **cloves garlic**, minced

¼–½ cup **butter**

shredded **cabbage** (if not using previously cooked)

cooked chopped vegetables: carrot, turnip, parsnip, potatoes, cabbage.

leftover **dressing**

leftover **turkey**, diced

1. There is no right or wrong way to make Bubble and Squeak. If you want to throw everything in the pan with some butter and fry it, turning it occasionally until you get some brown crispy bits, that's perfectly fine. Enjoy!

2. If I'm serving it to guests, I like to take a more structured approach so it presents well on the plate. I begin by cooking the onions and garlic in the butter over medium heat until they soften but do not brown. Cabbage is a pretty essential ingredient to Bubble and Squeak, so if I have not cooked it previously, I add about 2 cups of shredded cabbage to the pan with the onions and garlic so it wilts and cooks along with them.

3. Remove this combination from the pan temporarily and add a little more butter if necessary.

4. Dice the leftover potatoes and cook them in the butter until they get some good colour on some of the sides, turning them occasionally. I find this makes a great base for the hash.

5. Add the onion and garlic mixture back to the pan along with all the other ingredients you are using and cook over medium-high heat. Turn every few minutes until the hash is hot and with plenty of browned edges on the potatoes and vegetables. Serve immediately with leftover gravy if you have it.

CELEBRATE THE
NEW YEAR

A new year deserves a great celebration, and these recipes will help you navigate it with ease. Whether you're throwing a big party or just having an intimate evening with close friends and family, my ideas for New Year's Nibbles are designed to deliciously impress with simple elegant bites.

New Year's dinner is traditionally a baked ham dinner for our family. It is still very much a celebration dinner but one that is a bit lower effort than the all-out expansive feast of the previous week. A well-glazed ham and a few flavourful side dishes is all you'll need to impress the crowd for New Year's Day dinner. After the revelry of the previous evening, keeping it simple is the best way to ensure a delicious start to the new year.

148
PARTRIDGEBERRY APPLE CHUTNEY

NEW YEAR'S HAM DINNER

Maple and Brown Sugar Glazed Ham

PREP TIME: **20** MINUTES | COOK TIME: **2** HOURS | SERVES **10** OR MORE WITH LEFTOVERS

A perfectly glazed ham is perhaps the ultimate example of the delicious flavour interaction when salty meets sweet. It's definitely the best example at any holiday season dinner. Whether your tradition is to cook ham on Christmas Eve, Christmas Day, New Year's Day, or any other time during the holidays, this simple recipe gets it just right.

I've always preferred a bone-in ham and a two-stage process for cooking it. The boiling stage keeps the meat moist, infuses flavour, and takes away any excess salt that's been used in the curing process. The baking stage locks in the juiciness and ensures the sticky, finger-licking glaze that everyone associates with a great baked ham. For me, both stages ensure a perfectly cooked ham you'll be proud to have as the centerpiece of your dinner table.

---

8 lb **bone-in smoked ham**

2 tbsp **peppercorns**

1 tbsp **whole cloves**

1 whole **star anise**

1 large **onion**, roughly chopped

2 **bay leaves**

1 cup **firmly packed brown sugar**

⅓ cup **pure maple syrup**

½ tsp **cinnamon** (optional)

¼ tsp **cloves** (optional)

1. Add the ham, peppercorns, cloves, star anise, onion, and bay leaf to a large stock pot. Make sure the ham is rind side down then cover almost completely with water.

2. Bring to a gentle boil and cook for 60 minutes.

3. Remove the ham from the stock and let it drain on a rack for a few minutes.

4. Remove the rind and most but not all of the fat underneath the rind. Leave about ½ inch of fat on top of the entire ham.

5. Score the fat with a sharp knife in a square or diamond pattern.

6. Let the ham steam off for about 15 minutes then pat it completely dry with paper towels. This helps the glaze to stick to the ham.

7. Preheat the oven to 400°F.

8. Mix together the brown sugar and maple syrup plus the cinnamon and cloves if you're using them. This mixture should resemble a semi-thick paste but should still flow just a little.

9. Place ham in a roasting pan and brush the top and sides of the ham with half of this paste.

10. Bake for 60 minutes. Brush on the glaze in two more increments 15 minutes apart during the cooking time.

11. Allow the ham to rest for 20 minutes before carving and serving.

Parmesan Garlic Potatoes Dauphinoise

PREP TIME: **20** MINUTES | COOK TIME: **60** MINUTES | SERVES **6**

Scalloped potatoes seem to be everyone's side dish of choice with ham. That doesn't mean they have to be boring though. Dauphinoise is essentially the French term for scalloped potatoes, so don't let that intimidate you; they're actually easier to prepare. Dauphinoise potatoes forego the step of making a white sauce in favour of letting indulgent, full-fat cream create the sauce in combination with the natural starch present in the potatoes. You can make endless varieties by changing up the herbs, the cheeses, or adding other flavour elements like Dijon mustard. This version keeps it simple with classic garlic, thyme, Parmesan, and a little mozzarella melted on top.

2 lbs peeled and sliced **yellow potatoes**

2 tbsp **butter**

2 **cloves garlic**, finely minced

2 cups **whipping cream**

½ cup **milk**

½ tsp **salt**

1 tbsp chopped **fresh thyme**

¾ cup **grated Parmesan cheese**

pinch **black pepper**

1½ cups **grated mozzarella cheese**

1. Preheat oven to 350°F. Grease a 10-inch round pie plate or 9x9-inch square baking dish with butter.

2. Peel the potatoes and slice them thinly.

3. In a large saucepan or Dutch oven, melt the butter and sauté the garlic for just a minute or so until it softens but does not brown.

4. Add the whipping cream, milk and salt to the softened garlic and gently bring to a slow simmer over medium heat.

5. Add the sliced potatoes and bring to a slow simmer once again. Simmer, uncovered, for 5 minutes.

6. Using a colander or coarse sieve, drain the potatoes but reserve the cream and milk mixture.

7. Arrange half of the potatoes in the bottom of the prepared baking dish. Sprinkle on a small pinch of black pepper, ½ of the chopped thyme, and half of the Parmesan cheese.

8. Pour half of the cream mixture over the potatoes.

9. Arrange the second half of the potatoes on top, followed by the pepper, thyme, Parmesan cheese, and cream mixture, as in the first layer.

10. Do not overfill the baking dish with the cream mixture. Make sure the liquid level is ½ inch below the top.

11. Sprinkle the mozzarella cheese on top.

12. Place the baking pan on a parchment-lined cookie sheet to catch any spill over that may occur and bake for approximately 60 minutes or until the top is a medium golden brown and the bubbling sauce appears to have thickened.

13. Let the potatoes rest for 10-15 minutes before serving.

Partridgeberry Apple Chutney

PREP TIME: **15** MINUTES | COOK TIME: **15** MINUTES | MAKES **2½–3** CUPS

1 small **red onion**, chopped

3 tbsp **extra virgin olive oil**

2 large **apples**, diced

½ tsp **kosher salt**

zest and **juice** of 1 **orange**

¼ cup **apple cider vinegar**

1 tbsp **finely grated ginger root**

1 cup **partridgeberries** (or small cranberries)

1 tsp **nutmeg**

pinch **ground cloves**

½ tsp **fresh coarsely ground black pepper**

3 tbsp **brown sugar**

pinch **red curry powder**, hot (optional)

Truth be told, this chutney is one we make year round to serve with pork chops, ham, roast pork, or even with chicken. The beautiful ruby-red colour makes it especially festive at the holidays. Since New Year's Day is very likely the final feast day of the season, it brings a welcome flash of brilliant holiday colour to the table while adding great tangy flavour to compliment the sweetly glazed baked ham. You just may find yourself making this year round as well.

1. Over medium-low heat, sauté the red onion in the olive oil for about 2 minutes until the onions become translucent but not browned.

2. Toss in the apples and sauté for an additional minute.

3. Add the remaining ingredients and simmer slowly, uncovered, for about 10 minutes until thickened to a chunky, jam-like consistency.

4. Leftovers can be stored in the refrigerator in a mason jar or other clean sealed container for several days.

Maple Spice Glazed Parsnip

PREP TIME: **10** MINUTES | COOK TIME: **30** MINUTES | SERVES **4**

Believe it or not, parsnips are pretty much a staple root vegetable at our house. The reason is simple: Spouse absolutely loves them. So we have them on hand for roasting with Sunday dinners or to add to one of her famous soups where their natural sweetness adds so much flavour to the broth.

We often oven roast many kinds of root vegetables from carrots to beets. This one adds a little sweet-spiced flavour to a vegetable that's a natural for oven roasting. The recipe can be adapted to use other vegetables as well, including carrots, turnip, or squash.

8 large **parsnips**, peeled and cut into sticks or slices

3 tbsp **olive oil**

salt and **pepper** to season

¼ cup **maple syrup**

pinch **ground cloves**

¼ tsp **cinnamon**

1. Preheat oven to 350°F.

2. Toss the parsnips in the olive oil and season with salt and pepper in a glass baking dish.

3. Bake for about 20 minutes then toss and bake for another 10 minutes or until the parsnips start to get fork tender.

4. Mix the maple syrup with the cloves and cinnamon, then add to the baking dish with the parsnips.

5. Roast for about another 15 minutes, tossing occasionally, until the parsnips are fully cooked. Serve immediately.

Peas *with* Shallot Thyme Butter

PREP TIME: **15** MINUTES | COOK TIME: **15** MINUTES | MAKES **2½–3** CUPS

4 cups **frozen peas**

⅓ cup **butter**

4 large or 6 small **shallots**, sliced

2 **cloves garlic**, minced

2 tsp **fresh thyme** or ½ tsp **dried thyme**

salt and **pepper** to season

2 or 3 **lemon wedges** (optional)

Side dishes are an important part of any holiday meal, but they need not be complicated to be delicious. This simple pea recipe is one I make in springtime and early summer when fresh peas are more readily available, but good-quality frozen peas can be substituted for a welcome reminder of Spring at your New Year's Day dinner. This is one of the dishes you'll want to make at the last minute before serving, but you can precook and chill the peas in the ice bath to save time. They'll make a bright, colourful addition to your celebration table.

1. Cook the frozen peas in boiling, lightly salted water for 4-5 minutes. Drain them and immediately plunge them into a large bowl of ice water to stop the cooking action and preserve their colour.

2. In a large non-stick pan, melt the butter and cook the shallots and garlic over medium-low heat until the shallots are softened but not browned.

3. Drain the peas from the ice water well, and add them to the pan along with the thyme, and lightly season with salt and pepper. Toss together over medium heat for just a few minutes to reheat the peas.

4. Serve with lemon wedges to squeeze over the peas if you like.

Bacon Cheddar Cornbread Muffins

PREP TIME: **15** MINUTES | COOK TIME: **15** MINUTES | MAKES **12**

¾ cup + 2 tbsp **all-purpose flour**

1 cup **yellow cornmeal**

2 tbsp **sugar**

1½ tsp **baking powder**

¼ tsp **baking soda**

2 large **eggs**

⅓ cup **melted butter**

1½ cups **buttermilk**
(or milk soured with 1-2 tbsp lemon juice)

6 slices **crisp-cooked bacon**, roughly chopped

¾ cup **grated cheddar cheese**
(or 3 oz cut in a 1-cm dice)

2 **green onions**, chopped

Most times I like to serve a cornbread stuffing with a baked-ham dinner. The stuffing usually has onions, herbs, and sometimes, cooked sausage, grated cheese, or even nuts to change it up; I'm always inventing new combinations of flavours.

When I'm pressed for time and have lots of other side dishes to prepare, like on New Year's Day, often a quick batch of cornbread muffins with bursts of flavour baked in is an easy alternative. Some guests and especially my son, Noah, often request them. Whatever the case, the plate is always empty at the end of the meal.

1.   Preheat oven to 350°F.

2.   Grease a 12-muffin pan very well.

3.   Sift together the flour, cornmeal, sugar, baking powder, and baking soda.

4.   Add the eggs, melted butter, and milk and beat together until smooth. Stir in the bacon, cheese, and green onion.

5.   Pour batter evenly into the greased muffin cups and bake for about 15-20 minutes or until a wooden toothpick inserted in the center comes out clean. Serve while still warm.

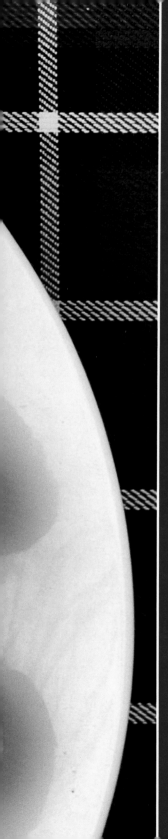

NEW YEAR'S NIBBLES

Garlic Thyme Cheese Puffs

PREP TIME: **30** MINUTES + CHILLING TIME | COOK TIME: **20** MINUTES | MAKES ABOUT **30**

CHOUX PASTRY SHELLS

1½ cups **water**

¾ cup **salted butter**

1½ cups **flour**

6 large **eggs**

CHEESE FILLING

8-10 **cloves roasted garlic** (about ½ a large bulb, you'll need a pinch of salt and pepper and a little drizzle of olive oil for this as well)

8 oz **goat cheese** (1 cup)

8 oz **cream cheese** (1 cup)

1 cup **whipping cream**

pinch **salt** and **pepper**

2 tsp finely chopped **fresh thyme**

You can use reduced-fat versions of cream cheese and/or goat cheese if you prefer. Low fat yogurt can be used as a substitute for the whipping cream as well. And if you don't like goat cheese, you can use all cream cheese in this recipe instead.

Some might say cheese puffs are a bit old fashioned for party food these days. I don't agree. It's another one of those standard recipes that should never go out of style because of its versatility. Start switching up the herbs or cheeses or add other flavour elements like toasted ground nuts and you have a brand new recipe. If empty trays are any indication, I've never served them at a party yet where they have not been some of the first finger foods to run out. It's another reason I always say, "Forget trendy; stick with tasty."

CHOUX PASTRY SHELLS

1. Add the water and butter to a medium-sized saucepan and bring to a gentle boil.

2. Reduce the heat to medium and quickly add the flour all at once, stirring quickly to form a soft dough.

3. Cook this mixture, stirring constantly, for an additional 3 minutes.

4. Allow this mixture to cool slightly for about 10-15 minutes, stirring occasionally, before adding the eggs, one at a time, and stirring until smooth after each addition.

5. Preheat oven to 425°F.

6. Drop the batter by rounded teaspoons (or pipe small mounds using a piping bag) onto a parchment-lined aluminum baking sheet.

7. Dip your finger in cold water and tap down the points at the top of the mounds of batter, especially if piping the batter. This helps to keep the tops rounded when baking.

8. Bake for 15 minutes, then reduce the heat to 375°F and bake for an additional 15-20 minutes until the puffs are golden brown and do not collapse when removed from the oven. These should be uniformly golden all over with no pale sides and sound hollow when tapped.

9. Cool completely on a wire rack

1. Preheat oven to 350°F.

2. To roast the half-bulb of garlic, cut a little off the top and place it on a square of aluminum foil. Drizzle with a teaspoon of olive oil and sprinkle with a pinch of salt and pepper.

3. Bring the four corners of the aluminum foil together and twist to seal the garlic in completely.

4. Roast the garlic in the oven for about 30 minutes until fully softened and golden.

5. Let it cool before removing the garlic from the skins and mashing it with a fork before using it in the filling.

6. Using an electric mixer, beat together the goat cheese and cream cheese until smooth.

7. Add mashed roasted garlic, whipping cream, pinch of salt and pepper, and thyme. Blend together until smooth.

8. Cover and refrigerate for 60 minutes or so before filling the choux pastry puffs.

9. Use a piping bag with a large open round or star tip to fill the cheese puffs. I prefer to half fill the puffs with the cheese filling. Filling them completely is too much of the rich filling for my taste.

10. Push the tip into the side of the cheese puff shell and squeeze about a rounded teaspoon of the filling inside.

11. If you do not have a piping bag, you can also split the cheese puff shells in half with a serrated knife and spoon the filling into the bottom half before putting them back together.

12. Chill until ready to serve.

Shrimp Cakes *with* Lime Aioli Dip

PREP TIME: **20** MINUTES | COOK TIME: **10** MINUTES | SERVES **6**

SHRIMP CAKES

½ lb coarsely chopped **fresh shrimp**

½ cup **cracker crumbs**

2 tbsp **mayonnaise**

½ tsp **lime zest**, minced

1 tsp **Worcestershire sauce**

¼ tsp **salt**

¼ tsp **pepper**

2 tsp **hot sauce** (optional) or pinch of chili flakes

1 **egg**, lightly beaten

1 tbsp chopped **cilantro**

⅓ cup **panko crumbs** + ⅓ cup **cracker crumbs** mixed

⅔ cup (approx.) **canola oil** for frying

LIME AIOLI DIP

1 **clove garlic**, finely minced

1 tsp **Dijon mustard**

1 large **egg yolk**

pinch **salt**

pinch **black pepper**

½ tsp finely minced **lime zest**

1 tbsp **lime juice**

½ cup **olive oil**

1 tbsp chopped **cilantro**

This is a great recipe for a small party with close friends. You can always double or triple the recipe for larger celebrations of course, but either way, getting a little prep work done in advance is always helpful. The aioli can be made earlier in the day and refrigerated, and you can always form the shrimp cakes, roll them in the crumbs, and chill them on a parchment-lined cookie sheet until ready to fry. Of course, if you are serving these first, you can always fry them and hold them in a warm oven for a half hour or so before your guests arrive.

SHRIMP CAKES

1. Be sure to coarsely chop (and not mince) the shrimp. Toss together the shrimp meat with the ½ cup cracker crumbs, mayonnaise, lime zest, Worcestershire sauce, salt, pepper, hot sauce, egg, and cilantro.

2. Form into 12 balls by hand. Roll in the additional cracker crumb/panko crumb mixture.

3. Heat about a half inch of canola oil in a skillet or sauté pan over medium-low heat. You want these to fry gently; they will burn quickly if the oil is too hot.

4. Fry until golden brown on both sides. Drain on paper towels.

LIME AIOLI DIP

1. Add the garlic, mustard, egg yolk, salt, pepper, lime zest and juice to a blender. Turn on the blender at medium to medium-high speed.

2. Pour in the olive oil very slowly in a thin, continuous stream until the aioli thickens. Pulse in the chopped cilantro at the end. Serve as a dip for the shrimp cakes.

Smoky Sweet Spiced Almonds

PREP TIME: **10** MINUTES | COOK TIME: **20** MINUTES | MAKES **2** CUPS

I've seen this recipe in several different versions using different spices over the years, but this one is my favourite sweet, spicy, and slightly salty version with smoky flavours from the chipotle and smoked paprika. They are perfect to set out as nibbles as your guests trickle in to the party. They also make terrific party favours or gifts. Fill some cellophane bags with them for your guests as they leave and include a copy of the recipe. Trust me, they're going to ask for it!

2 cups **whole raw almonds**

1 tbsp **melted butter**

3 tbsp **brown sugar**

½ tsp **ground cinnamon**

¾ tsp **chili powder**

½ tsp **cayenne pepper**

1 tsp **smoked paprika**

½ tsp **chipotle powder**

1½ tbsp **maple syrup**

1 tsp **kosher salt**

1. Preheat oven to 350°F.

2. Place the almonds on a parchment-lined cookie sheet and bake for 5 minutes. Toss them around and bake for another 5 minutes.

3. Allow to cool for a few minutes while you prepare the coating.

4. In a medium-sized bowl, mix the remaining ingredients together well.

5. Toss the warm nuts in the mixture until evenly coated, then roast on a parchment-lined baking sheet for 12-18 minutes, depending on the size of the nuts to get them perfectly toasted.

6. Watch them carefully and toss them around several times during the baking time to make sure they stay separate and don't clump together.

7. Allow them to cool on the pan for at least 10 minutes before serving.

8. Continue to toss them several times as they cool to keep the nuts separated.

9. When completely cool, these can be stored in an airtight container for up to a week or so.

Parmesan Marinara Baked Mussels

PREP TIME: **20** MINUTES | COOK TIME: **15** MINUTES | MAKES **24**

These mussels, served on the half-shell, are always a hit whenever I serve them, which is often as a first course at dinner, but they make elegant hors d'oeuvres too. They are very easy to prepare in advance and store on a baking sheet in the fridge until ready to pop in the oven. You can use your own favourite recipe for marinara sauce for these or just use a good-quality jarred brand. These really are impressive to serve but not nearly as fussy to make as your guests will probably think.

24 **large mussels**

1 cup **marinara sauce**

⅓ cup **melted butter**

3 **cloves garlic**, minced

1½ cups **crusty bread crumbs**

1 tsp chopped **fresh thyme**

pinch **coarsely ground black pepper**

⅓ cup **finely grated Parmesan cheese**

1. Wash the mussels and pull off any beards still attached to the shell. A pair of needle-nose pliers works well for this. Discard any mussels with cracked or broken shells and those that do not remain closed after a minute when you pinch them together. Also discard any mussels that do not open during the cooking time.

2. Bring 1 inch of water to a boil in a large covered pot. Add the mussels, cover the pot, and let them steam for only 3 minutes to open the shells.

3. Remove the top shell and loosen the mussels from the half of the shells that they are attached to before laying them in a baking dish.

4. Spoon about a teaspoon of marinara sauce over each mussel in their shell.

5. Over medium heat, melt the butter in a small saucepan and add the garlic. Cook for just a minute to soften it.

6. Add the bread crumbs, chopped thyme, and black pepper. Stir to combine well, then toss in the Parmesan cheese.

7. Preheat oven to 375°F.

8. Spoon the crumbs evenly over the marinara sauce-covered mussels. Press the crumbs down gently and bake for 15 minutes. Serve immediately.

Strawberry Balsamic Goat Cheese Bruschetta

PREP TIME: **15** MINUTES | COOK TIME: **15** MINUTES | MAKES ABOUT **12**

1 tbsp **olive oil**

1 **shallot**, chopped

½ **clove garlic**, minced

2 cups quartered **ripe strawberries**

1-2 tsp **honey**

pinch **salt**

¼ tsp **ground thyme**

½ tsp **ground cinnamon**

½ tsp **freshly ground black pepper**

1½ tbsp **balsamic vinegar**

12 toasted slices of **baguette**

4 oz **goat cheese**

This recipe takes strawberries to the savoury side while retaining some of their natural sweetness to balance the other robust flavours in the chutney and in the goat cheese. It is an unusually delicious combination of flavours that's bound to surprise and delight at any party. If fresh strawberries are not available, don't hesitate to use frozen, the end result will be equally delicious.

1. In a non-stick sauté pan, over medium heat, add the olive oil, chopped shallot, and garlic.

2. Sauté just until the shallot is softened but not browned.

3. Add the strawberries, honey, salt, thyme, cinnamon, and pepper.

4. Sauté together over medium-high heat until the mixture reaches a thick jam-like consistency.

5. In the last couple of minutes of cooking time, stir in the balsamic vinegar.

6. Taste the chutney in the last minute of cooking. If it is too sweet, you can add a little more balsamic vinegar; if too sour, add a little more honey to taste.

7. Serve on toasted baguette pieces along with a teaspoon or so of goat cheese.

Mushroom Pâté Bruschetta
with Seared Scallops

PREP TIME: **15** MINUTES | COOK TIME: **25** MINUTES | MAKES ABOUT **1½** CUPS PÂTÉ

This recipe is one I refer to as the "Land & Sea" of party food. The land is represented by the earthy, intense flavour of the mushrooms and thyme. The delicate flavour of the sea is represented in the succulent, pan-seared scallops. These elements are so very different from each other, but work so deliciously well together.

This is also a two-for-one recipe in that the mushroom pâté stands up deliciously on its own, to serve on slices of baguette or with crackers. It's a great vegetarian party-food option too. You can use any mushrooms you like in this recipe or use a combination of types like cremini and shitake to add even more depth of flavour.

3 tbsp **butter**

2 **cloves garlic**, minced

1 cup finely diced **shallots**

2 cups finely chopped **mushrooms**

1 tsp chopped **fresh thyme**
(or ½ tsp dry thyme)

pinch **salt** and **pepper** to season

½ cup **white wine**

½ cup finely ground **toasted pecans**

¼ cup **soft butter**

toasted slices of **baguette**

pan-seared, medium-sized **scallops**

1. Melt the butter in a sauté pan over medium heat.

2. Add the garlic and shallots and sauté for only a few minutes until the shallots soften but do not brown.

3. Add the mushrooms, thyme, salt, and pepper and cook until the mushrooms have shrunken and are just beginning to brown. Add the white wine and reduce until the liquid has practically cooked off.

4. Let the mushroom mixture cool to room temperature before adding it to a food processor along with the ground toasted pecans.

5. Process for a few minutes until the pâté is completely smooth, then pulse in the softened butter until well combined and smooth.

6. Transfer the pâté to a serving dish, cover with plastic wrap, and chill for several hours before serving.

7. To make the bruschetta, simply toast small slices of baguette under the broiler. Top with a little of the mushroom pâté and finally medium-sized scallops that have been lightly pan-seared in butter.

ACKNOWLEDGEMENTS

This cookbook is a work of reminiscence for me as I am reminded of the many family Christmases of my upbringing, and those more recently with my own children. Family is at the heart of this book; it is where I learned that Christmas is more about sharing the occasion with those you love most.

Thanks to the many great cooks and bakers in my extended family who taught me so much over the years. So much of the inspiration for this book comes from them.

Thanks to all of my loyal followers online and the many thousands of people who actually purchased my first two cookbooks. Your continued support and encouragement is the reason this book even exists.

Thanks once again to the entire team at Breakwater Books, especially to my editor James Langer, who ensures that what I write makes sense, and to Rhonda Molloy, whose design inspiration brings my work beautifully to life.

As always, thanks to Lynn, Olivia, and Noah, who still make me anticipate Christmas like a kid.

INDEX

One wife, two kids, one mortgage, lifelong food obsessive, recipe blogger, and food photographer: that's how *Rock Recipes* creator Barry C. Parsons describes himself on *RockRecipes.com*. Called "one of the best food blogs in Canada" by the *National Post*, *Rock Recipes* boasts over half a million followers from around the world. The popularity of his recipes and cooking philosophy has led to two incredibly successful cookbooks: *Rock Recipes: The Best Food from My Newfoundland Kitchen* and *Rock Recipes 2: More Great Food and Photos from My Newfoundland Kitchen*. Parsons lives in St. John's, Newfoundland.

f /RockRecipes   🐦 @RockRecipes   📌 /RockRecipes

Hazelnut Coconut Fruitcake

PREP TIME: **30** MINUTES + CHILLING TIME | COOK TIME: UP TO **2½** HOURS | MAKES ABOUT **3** DOZEN

If you're like me when shopping for Christmas baking supplies, you probably have a tendency to overbuy as well. This particular fruitcake recipe came about one year as a way for me to use whatever was left over from other Christmas baking projects. I actually used a pound-cake recipe base and added all the other ingredients to it. It turned out wonderfully and, unlike darker fruitcakes, need not be made well in advance. That makes it a perfect last-minute fruitcake idea too. Not bad for a cupboard cleaner recipe!

1½ cups **butter**

2 cups **sugar**

3 **eggs**

1 tsp **vanilla extract**

1 tsp **coconut extract**

½ tsp **almond extract** (optional)

3 cups **flour** + ¼ cup to dredge the fruit

1½ tsp **baking powder**

1 cup undiluted **evaporated milk**

2 cups **glacé cherries**

¾ cup **glacé mixed citrus peel**

1 cup chopped **glacé pineapple**

1 cup roughly chopped, **toasted hazelnuts**

1 cup fine-cut **dried coconut**

1½ cups **light or golden raisins**

4–8 oz of **light rum, coconut rum, or brandy**

1. Preheat oven to 300°F.

2. Cream together the butter and sugar well.

3. Add the eggs, one at a time, beating well after each addition until light and fluffy.

4. Beat in the vanilla, coconut, and almond extracts.

5. Sift together the 3 cups of flour and baking powder.

6. Fold dry ingredients into the creamed mixture alternately with the evaporated milk, beginning and ending with the dry ingredients. As a general rule, I add the dry ingredients in 3 portions and the milk in 2 portions.

7. Toss all of the dried fruit with the ¼ cup of flour and fold into the batter well along with the chopped nuts and the dried coconut.

8. Bake in greased and floured springform pan, tube pan, or loaf pans lined with parchment paper. Bake for 1½ to 2½ hours, depending upon the size of your pan (see note below).

There is a total of 2½ lbs of nuts and dried or glacé fruit in this recipe. You can substitute other dried fruits if you like. Baking time will depend on the size and shape of pan you use. I used a 10-inch springform pan which takes the longest at about 2½ hours. A large tube or funnel pan should take about 2 hours because of the shape. Watch it carefully after the first 1½ hours of baking time and take it out of the oven only when a toothpick inserted in the center comes out completely clean.